Who's That in the White House?

The Founding Years

1789 to 1829

GEORGE
WASHINGTON

JOHN
ADAMS

THOMAS
JEFFERSON

JAMES
MADISON

JAMES
MONROE

JOHN QUINCY
ADAMS

by Rose Blue and Corinne J. Naden

RSVP
RAINTREE
STECK-VAUGHN
PUBLISHERS
The Steck-Vaughn Company

Austin, Texas

To the memory of Mary Lee Graeme and to Rose's mom,
two very gutsy ladies.

Published by Raintree Steck-Vaughn Publishers, an imprint of Steck-Vaughn Company

Publishing Director: Walter Kossmann
Project Manager: Lyda Guz
Editor: Shirley Shalit
Photo Editor: Margie Foster
Electronic Production: Scott Melcer
Consultant: Andrew Frank, University of Florida

Library of Congress Cataloging-in-Publication Data
Blue, Rose.
The founding years 1789 to 1829 / by Rose Blue and Corinne J. Naden.
p.   cm. — (Who's that in the White House?)
Includes bibliographical references and index.
Summary: Discusses the political lives and times of the first six United States presidents, as well as general information about the presidency.
ISBN 0-8172-4300-3
1. Presidents — United States — Biography — Juvenile literature.   2. United States — Politics and government — 1789-1815 — Juvenile literature.   3. United States — Politics and government — 1815-1861 — Juvenile literature.   [1. Presidents.]   I. Naden, Corinne J. II. Title.   III. Series.
E176.1.B67   1998
973'.09'9 — dc21   97-14218
                                                                                      CIP   AC

Acknowledgments
The authors wish to thank Harold C. Vaughan of Fort Lee, New Jersey,
for his critical reading of the manuscript.

Photography credits: Cover White House Photo; Title page (all) National Portrait Gallery, Smithsonian Institution; p. 4 White House Photo; p. 6 Susan Biddle/White House Photo; p. 7 White House Photo; p. 8 National Portrait Gallery, Smithsonian Institution; pp. 11, 14, 15, 19 The Granger Collection; p. 24 National Portrait Gallery, Smithsonian Institution; pp. 25, 27, 29, 31 The Granger Collection; p. 35 National Portrait Gallery, Smithsonian Institution; p. 37 Corbis-Bettmann; pp. 38, 39, 41, 44 The Granger Collection; p. 45 Corbis-Bettmann; p. 46 (top left, right) The Granger Collection, (bottom left) Corbis-Bettmann; p. 50 National Portrait Gallery, Smithsonian Institution; pp. 51, 56, 58, 59 The Granger Collection; p. 62 National Portrait Gallery, Smithsonian Institution; pp. 63, 67, 69, 71 The Granger Collection; p. 74 National Portrait Gallery, Smithsonian Institution; p. 75 The Granger Collection; p. 76 National Museum of American Art, Smithsonian Institution; pp. 81, 82 Corbis-Bettmann.

Cartography: GeoSystems, Inc.

Printed and bound in the United States
1 2 3 4 5 6 7 8 9 0 LB 01 00 99 98 97

Contents

Prologue

The Office of President of the United States

"What do you want to be when you grow up?"

*H*ow many times have you been asked that question? Have you ever answered "President of the United States"? Some people say it's the best job ever. Others say it's the worst. Lots of people say it's the hardest. But most everyone agrees that now, in the late twentieth century, it's the most powerful job in the world.

From the birth of the nation to the present day, Washington to the man in the White House today, the United States has had 42 Presidents. However, only 41 different people—all men so far—have actually held the job. That's because Grover Cleveland was elected as both the twenty-second and the twenty-fourth

The White House seen from the rear, as it appears today.

Presidents of the United States. Of all the Presidents, only George Washington, the first, never called the White House his home. He never lived there at all. Franklin Delano Roosevelt occupied the Oval Office the longest: 12 years and 39 days, beginning in 1933. William Henry Harrison wasn't so lucky back in 1841. His term was the shortest. Harrison died of pneumonia less than 31 days after taking office.

Presidents have been fairly young (John Kennedy was 43 on Inauguration Day) and fairly old (Ronald Reagan was 78 when he left office). By far, the largest number (24) have been lawyers, but we've also had generals (Ulysses S. Grant, for instance), a teacher (James Garfield), a tailor (Andrew Johnson), a journalist (Warren Harding), and an actor (Ronald Reagan).

The responsibilities of the President are awesome, and the major ones are clearly defined in the U.S. Constitution. Strangely enough, the Articles of Confederation, which served as the first constitution after the American Revolution, did not provide for a chief executive. And since each of the colonies had had its own governor with no one in charge over all, the leaders of the new country were treading on unfamiliar ground.

The President's chief duties are to make sure that all laws are faithfully carried out. This is done through agencies and departments of the government. The President nominates federal judges, including those who sit on the Supreme Court, subject to the "advice and consent" of the U.S. Senate. The President appoints members of the Cabinet and most of the high-ranking officials in the executive branch of government. The Cabinet is made up of presidential advisers who are also generally the heads of departments, such as the Department of State or the Treasury. Appointing his own advisers, with Senate approval, is a power of the President not defined in the Constitution. It has grown by custom through the years. In peace and war, the President is Commander in Chief of all U.S. armed forces. With Senate approval, the President has the power to make treaties with foreign governments. The President can approve or reject—veto—bills passed by Congress. That is great power and great responsibility placed in the hands of one individual.

The Oval Office and the President's desk as they appeared in 1990 when George Bush inhabited the White House.

Considering the responsibilities of the job, the President of the United States doesn't make a lot of money. Sitting behind that huge desk in the Oval Office will earn a yearly salary of $200,000, plus a $50,000 expense account. A superstar baseball player makes several million dollars a year, and so does the president of a large corporation.

If money isn't the top priority for those who seek the White House, what is? There is prestige. People stand up when you enter a room, and they rush to fulfill your every wish. There is power. As head of one of the world's mightiest and wealthiest nations, you can change history by the decisions you make. But that wasn't always so. In the early years, the rest of the world wasn't much impressed by the leader of a very young and weak United States.

Maybe there is something else important for those who seek the White House. Perhaps it is the office itself. Some of our Presidents were great statesmen, some were not. Some were strong and honest. Others were not so. Some worked hard for the United States. Some did very little. But all in all, as a group, they have done well in guiding a nation through the pains of growth, expansion, wars, disasters, and a constantly changing world. There have been many changes through the years in the way the men who have held this office have handled the job. But in general, the first six Presidents, the men covered in this book, have all been concerned primarily with following the U.S. Constitution and preserving the promise that began with the American Revolution.

The books in the "Who's That in the White House?" series will show how the country grew during different administrations and perhaps how the President grew, too. Often through the years, the man who sat in the White House changed the history of the United States. That was probably never more true than during the terms of the first six Presidents covered in this volume. But very often, the job changed the man as well.

This is the story of that very special group of very different people who are united by a common address: 1600 Pennsylvania Avenue, Washington, D.C.—the White House. *The Founding Years* introduces six extraordinary individuals, including the first and probably most well-known President and the only father-son combination to take the office so far. Jefferson is surely the leader with the widest scope of interests and skills. Madison, the shortest of the Presidents, became a giant of democracy. Monroe was the last of the towering eighteenth-century figures to lead the nation and the third U.S. President to die on the Fourth of July.

The Great Seal of the President of the United States. The country's motto, which also appears on many coins— E pluribus unum, is Latin for "one made out of many," referring to one nation made of many states.

George Washington (1789-1797)

Simply because he was the first, George Washington had a great and lasting impact on the office of President of the United States. Everything he did or thought about the presidency influenced, more or less, those who followed him. But Washington's own character had great and lasting impact, too. He was very aware of the power of his office. He believed a President should act strictly according to the Constitution. He believed a President should appoint the best people, regardless of differing viewpoints. He believed the office of President should be above politics. And, in fact, he himself was a reserved man who sometimes acted "above the rough and tumble of government." This often annoyed those who worked with and admired him. The first vice president, John Adams, once got so irked at Washington's icy calm that he called him an "old mutton head."

Aloof he might have been, perhaps indeed an old mutton head, but George Washington was everybody's choice for first President of the United States. That is, the choice of everyone in the Electoral College, for those were the men who voted. The new Constitution included a new device—the Electoral College. The delegates to the Constitutional Convention of 1787 were not pleased with the thought of having a President elected by popular vote. Wouldn't that make him more likely to try to please the crowds instead of govern the country? But if popular vote wasn't the answer, what was? The delegates compromised on the Electoral College. Each state would have the same number of electors as it had members in both the Senate and the House of Representatives. Each state could decide how to choose its own electors, and they—not the people in general—would vote for President. The person who got the most votes would be President, the person with the next highest number would be vice president, although the ballot did not actually list those offices. This brought on a sticky problem in 1800 because Thomas Jefferson and Aaron Burr, on the Democratic-Republican ticket, each got the same number of votes. Suddenly, the nation had two Presidents! The election was thrown into the House of Representatives, which picked Jefferson. Four years later, a constitutional amendment declared that electors must name a person for a specific office, such as Jefferson for President, Burr for vice president.

The popular vote for President wasn't even counted until the election of John Quincy Adams in 1824. How times change. In the latter part of the twentieth century, there have been many rumblings about doing away with the Electoral College entirely and just choosing the President on popular vote alone.

Why did the electors vote as they did? Why Washington? The answer, of course, lies in the time, the circumstances, and the man.

George Washington was born in Westmoreland County, in the British colony of Virginia, on the morning of February 11, 1732. When the modern calendar was adopted 20 years later, his birthdate became February 22.

George's parents were Augustine and Mary Ball Washington. His father was a gentle man, but his mother was a testy woman. In later life she resented her eldest son's success, and she would not go to any ceremonies that honored him. George also had three brothers, two sisters, two half brothers, and one half sister. His father died when George was 11, and the boy then looked on his much-older half brother Lawrence as a father figure. George received the rather irregular education common to the colony at the time, picking up basic reading, writing, and math. He did not attend a university. When he was 16, he moved to his brother's estate up the Potomac River at Epsewasson, now known as Mount Vernon.

In his teenage years, people couldn't help but notice George Washington. At a time when the average man and woman were a good deal shorter than today, young George was six foot two and lanky. He had brown hair, gray-blue eyes, and big feet. His shoes were size 13. He was graceful, quiet, and an excellent horseman like most of the Virginia gentry of the time. When he was 19, he came down with smallpox, which left his face pitted and scarred. But the pockmarks were good luck charms in disguise. He was now immune to the disease that killed many soldiers in the Continental Army during the American Revolution.

In 1749, Washington did some surveying work in Culpepper County, Virginia, and three years later inherited Mount Vernon after the death of his half brother Lawrence. That same year, at age 20, he became a major in the Virginia militia. He spent the next two years defending the Virginia frontier against the French in the French and Indian War. After one of his first battles, he wrote that the sound of whistling bullets had a "certain charm." He changed his mind, however, when four bullets pierced his coat, but not his chest, and two horses were shot out from under him.

Washington retired from the military in 1758 when he was elected to the Virginia House of Burgesses, the colony's governing body under the royal governor. He served for 15 years. In 1759, he married perhaps the richest widow in the Virginia colony, Martha Dandridge Custis. Friendly and plump, Martha had two children, a town house in Williamsburg, the colonial capital, 17,000 acres of land, and 300 slaves. Washington himself had 49 slaves at the time and 5,000 acres of land. The future President's attitude about slavery was the common one: Slaves were property and he could not see a future without them.

A youthful George Washington without a white wig is shown in this lithograph being married to Martha Dandridge Custis on January 6, 1759.

Although he did not hold slavery itself as evil, as the years passed, he began to see the evils brought on by the slave trade and approved laws that would do away with it. This was an attitude common among many southerners. The slave trade was wrong; slavery itself was not.

Martha, whom Washington called Patsy, and George settled down at Mount Vernon where he became a tobacco planter. He also got involved in the events that led to the American Revolution. He was angry when the British closed the port of Boston after the colonists had dumped tea into the harbor rather than pay the tea tax. He met with Thomas Jefferson and others in a Williamsburg tavern after the British dissolved the House of Burgesses. They vowed that if the British attacked one colony, it would be regarded as an attack on all of them. In 1774, Washington attended the First Continental Congress in Philadelphia, where the colonists decided what actions to take against the British rulers. And at the Second Continental

Congress, in May 1775, John Adams of Massachusetts suggested George Washington as Commander in Chief of the forming Continental Army.

On July 4, 1776, the Thirteen Colonies announced their separation from Great Britain with the Declaration of Independence. It stated the American ideal of government and is perhaps the most important of all U.S. historical documents.

Washington had both success and failure fighting the British until they surrendered on October 17, 1781. He was forced to retreat many times against superior British forces, but he had victories as well. On Christmas night 1776, he and his men rowed across the Delaware River and caught the British by surprise at Trenton, New Jersey. He surprised them again at nearby Princeton, where he cut off the enemy's supply lines. But he lost more than 1,000 men at Germantown, Pennsylvania, on October 4, 1777, and retreated in lonely defeat to a dreary and terrible winter at Valley Forge.

What kind of commander was George Washington? Some say he made too many mistakes. He was too slow in making decisions. He was too indecisive. Others say none of that mattered. After all, he won. And that was no small feat. His troops were very poorly trained and undisciplined. They were mostly short-term members of the colonial militias and didn't want to be in the army at all. Yet, Washington took them into the field against crack British regulars and Hessian (German) paid soldiers—and they won. It is said that much of the credit for his troops' survival during the terrible winter at Valley Forge was due to Washington's confidence in their eventual success.

George Washington became a hero. He retired in 1783 at the age of 51 to be a "private citizen on the banks of the Potomac." However, his private life did not last long. In 1781, the Articles of Confederation had been established to govern the new country. But the new Congress had no power to enforce taxes or requests for troops. Nor did the Articles give the country a central leader.

It was soon clear that a strong and effective constitution was needed. So, in 1787, George Washington was back in politics as a delegate to the Constitutional Convention in Philadelphia. The original purpose was to revise the rather weak Articles of Confederation. But James Madison and other Virginia delegates argued strongly for an entirely new constitution. They presented the Virginia Plan, drawn up by Madison and representing the interests of the larger states. After much revision and debate, and compromise with the smaller states, it became the basis for the U.S. Constitution.

Washington was chosen president of the convention. He made one speech, voted for giving the leader of the new government strong powers, and went back to Mount Vernon.

The Constitution of the United States was ratified (approved) by the required nine states on June 21, 1788. The following February, Washington got the word at Mount Vernon. The Electoral College had named him the new nation's first President. All the electors, a total of 69, had voted for him. At that time, the electors voted for two men on the same ballot. The man with the second highest number of votes became the nation's first vice president. He was John Adams of Massachusetts, who had received 34 electoral votes.

Political parties as we know them today were not organized in those early years. In fact, Washington did not favor the formation of political parties. However, because he favored a strong central government, Washington is known as a Federalist. Those not in favor of a strong central government were anti-Federalists or, later, Jeffersonian Republicans.

Upon his election in 1789, the new nation's first President was 57 years old. He was about to lead a great experiment in democracy.

Washington took his election and his responsibilities with dignity and seriousness. Perhaps his manner helped the new Congress to decide just what they should call him. There was

George Washington standing with his hand on the Bible is shown here being inaugurated as the first President of the United States at Federal Hall in New York City, April 30, 1789.

much debate over the title of this new office. Some of the senators suggested such names as "His Elective Majesty," "His Highness," and even "His Mightiness." These sounded too much like another king to many, however. A more rational solution came from the House of Representatives. George Washington would be called simply "President of the United States."

Dressed in a brown suit and white silk stockings, Washington, his dress sword at his side, took the oath of office in New York City on April 30, 1789. All Presidents who have followed Washington have taken that same oath. As the new chief executive bent to kiss the Bible, Robert Livingston, chancellor of New York, shouted, "Long live George Washington, President of the United States!"

Washington tried hard to maintain what he considered to be the dignity of his new office. He refused to accept a salary and asked only for expenses. He appointed people regardless of their political beliefs if he thought them truly qualified. That is why author of the Declaration of Independence and anti-Federalist Thomas Jefferson became the first secretary of state, and Federalist Alexander Hamilton, the President's former military aide and a financial genius, was named the first secretary of the treasury.

Strictly speaking, George Washington should not be included in a series that asks "Who's That in the White House?" He never lived there. But in 1791, from the temporary capital in Philadelphia, Washington appointed commissioners to supervise the building of a new capital city. Taken from land in Maryland and Virginia, it was to be called the District of Columbia. The President chose Benjamin Banneker, a black mathematician, to survey the site. A Frenchman who served in the Continental Army, Pierre Charles L'Enfant, was chosen to design the city, government buildings, and "President's Palace."

Washington was pleased with L'Enfant's design for the "palace," but most everyone else thought it much too royal. So, in 1792 the President agreed to Jefferson's idea for a competition to design the "President's House." The winner, selected by Washington, was James Hoban, an Irish architect, who proposed a handsome three-story, stone building. Hoban won $500 and a gold medal.

The first President knew he would never live in the White House. Nevertheless, he thought the design was too small for future occupants and their families, so he had it enlarged by one-fifth. This and other changes boosted the final cost to about $300,000. It would not be finished until the administration of the second President of the United States, John Adams. Almost from the start, the building came to be called simply the White House for the color of its exterior stone.

This woodcut of Benjamin Banneker appeared originally on the title page of Banneker's Almanack, 1795.

Washington wanted competence and simplicity in the office of the President. Yet, he well understood the power that his position gave him. He knew, and sometimes even said, that the things he did would set the rule for all those who followed. He was not above using the presidency in a way that would bring honor, not to himself, but to the office. For instance, when he was visiting Massachusetts early in his administration, he got an invitation to "come see" the governor, John Hancock. Washington quickly let the governor know just "who should call on whom." Hancock received a note saying that the "President of the United States" would be "at home, 'till 2 o'clock." To this day, even the most important national figures call on the President, not the other way around.

By the end of his first four years in office, Washington was ready to go home. He really didn't much like being President. He longed for the peace of Mount Vernon where he could "amuse myself in agriculture." But Jefferson and Hamilton implored him to stay for the good of the country. Naturally, he gave in, even though these two—who constantly quarreled—were mainly the ones who were giving him a difficult time.

When the new government was formed, Washington was strongly against political parties. He wanted to avoid the squabbling that he had seen in England and in the colonies prior to independence. He was convinced that such infighting was the very thing that could bring down a new and fragile government.

So what did he do? He brought into his first Cabinet two of the strongest, most learned, dedicated, and brilliant men of his day. And what did they do? Alexander Hamilton and Thomas Jefferson immediately disagreed on almost every major issue. They didn't like each other personally, and they couldn't stand each other politically. Hamilton stood for a strong central government. A financial wizard, his interests were with the business community and the North. Jefferson, an aristocrat of the South and backer of agricultural interests, saw a strong federal government as a real threat to liberty. Hamilton said Jefferson was "cautious and sly." Jefferson said Hamilton was trying to replace the new republican government with an old-style monarchy.

Washington's temperament and their respect for him might have kept Hamilton and Jefferson from actual blows, but their constant war of words disturbed the President. So, when Jefferson and Hamilton agreed to quiet the mudslinging, in public at least, Washington agreed to a second term.

Washington also had some peacekeeping problems with his vice president. John Adams believed himself more brilliant than Washington, Jefferson, and Hamilton combined and generally disliked everybody else. With these three personalities in his administration, Washington's true genius becomes apparent. Could anyone else at that place and time have done so well in holding together the infant government and the strong-willed men who had separate and powerful ideas about which way the country should be run?

Washington was elected unanimously to a second term in 1792, with 132 electoral votes. Adams was again vice president, with 77 votes. Washington's second administration was tested by three events that clearly show how he put his personal stamp on U.S. history.

There was the Citizen Genêt affair. In 1793, young Edmond-Charles Genêt arrived in Charleston, South Carolina, as a French minister to the U.S. government. At this time, France and England were at war. Washington thought it in America's best interests to remain neutral. However, Genêt privately outfitted several vessels and recruited some Charleston ship captains to sail them.

The usually placid Washington was furious. He warned the fanatic Frenchman to stop. But Genêt was impressed with his own success. Egged on by the growing number of anti-British Americans who called him "Citizen Genêt," he marched in triumph from Charleston to Philadelphia. According to John

Adams, "Ten thousand people in the streets of Philadelphia... threatened to drag Washington out of his house and effect a revolution...."

Hamilton was afraid the new government might topple, and even pro-French Jefferson was upset. Finally, Washington had had enough. He demanded that the French recall their firebrand minister. Alas for Genêt, the government that had sent him to America was no longer in power. Execution in eighteenth-century France was often via the infamous *guillotine*, which looked rather like an enormous paper cutter. The possibility of having his head chopped off if he went home began to seem all too real. Citizen Genêt may have been a fanatic, but he was not stupid. He begged the U.S. President for forgiveness and asylum. With order restored, Washington relented. Genêt indeed became Citizen Genêt. He married the daughter of the governor of New York, retired into obscurity on a farm, and died in 1834.

Another test of leadership involved John Jay, first Chief Justice of the U.S. Supreme Court (1789). By 1794, the United States and Great Britain were close to war again. The British had been seizing U.S. ships and impressing, or forcing, some American sailors into the Royal Navy. In addition, Great Britain still had troops in the Northwest Territory. This was the land south of the Great Lakes between the Mississippi and Ohio Rivers. By treaty, it now belonged to the United States, but the British government was inciting Native Americans to fight against U.S. settlements there.

Urged by Hamilton, Washington sent Chief Justice Jay to England to calm things down. The Treaty of London, sometimes called Jay's Treaty, was signed in November 1794 but not made public until the following March. America did not do particularly well by the treaty. England agreed to get out of the Northwest Territory and at least to talk about payment for the American ships they had seized. Not a word, however, was said about impressing U.S. sailors or inciting Native Americans to fight.

Worse still, the U.S. government didn't get what it really wanted. It wanted the British to allow Americans to reopen the profitable trade with the British West Indies, banned since the Revolution. Great Britain agreed, but included so many trade restrictions as to make resumption of trade a joke.

When the public heard about the terms of the treaty, they were outraged! Reject it, they cried! The British are toying with us! The Senate began to make noises about not signing. Washington didn't like the treaty any more than anyone else. He knew that to sign it would be embarrassing to America. He also knew that to reject it might mean war. He urged the Congress to sign the treaty, which it did—without much enthusiasm. The vote in favor was 20 to 10.

Washington's move was unpopular but wise. It kept a young and weak United States out of a war it probably could not have won. The British finally left the Northwest Territory in 1796, and relations between the two countries improved. Washington had kept his patience—and may have saved his country.

Then, there was the Whiskey Rebellion. Prompted by Hamilton, Congress passed a new tax bill in 1791. The government needed money, but Hamilton thought taxes on business were high enough. His bill put a tax on a domestic product—whiskey.

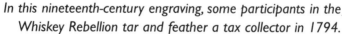

In this nineteenth-century engraving, some participants in the Whiskey Rebellion tar and feather a tax collector in 1794.

This did not sit well with farmers. It especially did not sit well with those farmers who were the small whiskey distillers in western Pennsylvania. They weren't happy about tax laws in general, but Hamilton's bill really made them mad. Whiskey was one of the top-selling products in the country. Surplus wheat, which was the main crop, although they raised corn and rye as well, was converted to whiskey. It was the farmers' main source of income. With the new tax at 25 cents on the dollar, that meant a lot of money out of their pockets and into the federal government's coffers.

The farmers began to grumble, loudly and a lot. Sometimes they even chased federal revenue officers off their land. Washington, as usual, remained patient. But in July 1794, the protest got ugly. In western Pennsylvania, about 500 armed farmers attacked and burned the home of a tax collector. Flushed with success, they threatened to march on Pittsburgh. Was this a test of the new government?

The President thought so. He warned the protesters to go home. When they didn't, he called out the state militia—15,000 strong. Then he rode out to review the troops himself, with Hamilton, the man the farmers most hated, at his side.

It was a quietly impressive show of government in action. The farmers fled. Washington was relieved. Some of the protesters were taken prisoner, but only two were tried for treason. Washington pardoned them both. He said one was crazy, and the other was simpleminded.

Jefferson and Hamilton were at each other's throats again. Jefferson was appalled by such a show of government force. Hamilton said the government had strengthened its reputation.

In these three events that so tested his young administration, President George Washington made a profound impact on the country. With his patience and genius for decision making, he proved that a leader could put the good of the nation above personal feelings. Washington had shown to all citizens, and to the world, that this young United States could and would enforce the laws on which its government was founded. It was a valuable lesson for a nation so young and still unsure of itself.

Washington's Farewell Address of 1796 is one of his most enduring legacies. He warned against the evils of "entangling alliances" abroad, urging America to stay out of Europe's problems. Isolationism was a strong part of U.S. foreign policy for the next century. He wasn't so successful, however, in warning against the evils of splitting into political parties. No sooner had he announced his retirement than Jefferson, as a Democratic-Republican, and Hamilton and Adams, under the Federalist banner, were battling each other. Washington would surely be astonished at the power of American political parties today!

After retirement, Washington, now 65, and Martha went home. Three years later, after being treated for a throat infection, he died on December 14, 1799. The country's first chief executive was buried at his beloved Mount Vernon, which is today a national historic landmark.

Because he was first, because he will forever be "the father of our country," George Washington has become perhaps larger than life. Americans remember him in many ways. The Washington Monument in the nation's capital is probably the most well known of any tribute to a U.S. President. Begun in 1848 and not finished until 1884, the obelisk, covered with white marble from Maryland, stands nearly 556 feet high. In respect to the first President, no building in the city can stand higher than the Washington Monument.

Washington's face is familiar to most Americans. Besides staring out from a one-dollar bill, his face is found in portraits and sculptures in countless public buildings. His likeness was probably captured in oil or in stone more than any other man of his time. The portraits show a serious, almost sad face, his skin pockmarked, his mouth somewhat distorted by his famous ill-fitting false teeth. Not a handsome face perhaps, but one full of trust and dignity.

The most famous myth about Washington is undoubtedly the cherry tree story. When asked if he had chopped down the tree, Washington said yes, because, according to the tale, he could not tell a lie. Thomas Jefferson said of Washington that his "mind was great and powerful, without being of the very first order...it was slow in operation, but sure in conclusion."

Washington's personal stamp forever influences the office of President of the United States. Perhaps more than any other who followed him, he tried to weigh the facts of any dispute fairly and honestly and to decide only on the basis of what was good and right for the country. Jefferson said that neither friendship nor hatred ever biased Washington's decisions. The first President believed that the leader of the United States must maintain the dignity of the office. He believed that the President must be firm where the Constitution was vague. For instance, the Constitution says nothing about naming a Cabinet. Washington named a strong one. But where the Constitution was clear, Washington also believed that the President should never stretch presidential powers or "relax from them."

It is never easy to be the first in uncharted waters. With honesty and patience, the new President tended the new nation, helped it to grow sturdy and strong, and nurtured the peace that its fledgling government promised.

Surely George Washington was the right man at the right place at the right time. Could any other have done as well? In his slow, quiet, determined, and serious way, he proved that the marvelous experiment in self-government, begun in 1789, could, indeed, work.

Names in the News in Washington's Time

Benjamin Franklin (1706–1790):

Boston-born statesman, scientist, philosopher, publisher of *Poor Richard's Almanack* (1732–1757). Member of the Second Continental Congress (1775); signer of the Declaration of Independence; negotiated treaty with France (1776) and with Great Britain (1781); member Constitutional Convention (1787). Invented improved heating stove (1744) and conducted famous electricity experiments with kites (1752).

Alexander Hamilton (1755–1804):

First secretary of the treasury. Probably the most dominant figure after the President. Brilliant and egotistical, his monetary policies established the Bank of the United States, which soon gave the young country a sound credit rating throughout the world and built confidence in the reliability of the new government. He is sometimes called the Father of Wall Street. Caribbean born, Kings College (now Columbia University) educated, he was killed in a duel with Aaron Burr. Long-time political rivals and enemies, Hamilton and Burr fought in Weehawken, New Jersey. Burr provoked the challenge over some nasty remarks Hamilton had supposedly written in a letter about him. The fatal duel left Hamilton's wife and seven children heavily in debt.

John Jay (1745–1829):

Born and educated in New York City, he was governor of New York from 1795 to 1801. First Chief Justice of the Supreme Court; sent by Washington to negotiate treaty with Great Britain (1794–1795).

Chapter Two

Four Years with Cranky John Adams

John Adams (1797-1801)

*T*he second President of the United States was a brilliant man and honest to the core. He was also unbearably vain and almost always cranky. Perhaps that was because he constantly worried about his health and felt that early death was just around the corner. In this he was wrong, for he lived to the age of 90.

John Adams did not make friends easily. Even those who admired him didn't always understand him. Benjamin Franklin said that Adams "means well for his country, is always an honest man, often a wise one, but sometimes, and in some things, is absolutely out of his senses." Alexander Hamilton went a step further, saying "there are great and intrinsic defects in his character which unfit him for the office of chief magistrate." Nevertheless, John Adams held himself so superior to everyone else that even those he agreed with weren't always sure whose side he was on! He did have a saving grace, however. He could be honest even about himself. In his diary, he acknowledged that he was "puffy and conceited." He probably never would have won an election in modern-day politics, which would have been a loss because Adams was a devoted, courageous, and brilliant patriot.

Young John's brilliance was slow to develop. Born on October 19, 1735, in Braintree (now Quincy), Massachusetts, he grew up enjoying work on his parents' colonial farm much more than going to school. Nevertheless, he entered Harvard in 1751, at the age of 16, and after graduation went into what was for him the worst possible career—teaching. He was so obviously shy and soft-spoken that his young pupils obeyed him not at all.

Luckily for Mr. Adams and the country, he left teaching for the practice of law in Braintree in 1758. It was there and then that he also met the love of his life. Abigail Smith might have been thought of as a feminist if the word had been invented in the eighteenth century. She was very smart, when women supposedly weren't. She read a lot, when women supposedly didn't. And in a time when women were often reminded to keep silent, Abigail Smith generally spoke her mind. She smiled at John's imagined illnesses and turned a conceited crank into a tender family man—at least at home. They were married in 1764, had three sons and two daughters, and remained loving partners all their lives.

John Adams may have been ineffective and shy as a teacher, but he turned out to be just the opposite as a lawyer. For example, on March 5, 1770, British soldiers and an unruly crowd of Bostonians came to blows. The soldiers killed five colonists in what became known as the Boston Massacre. They were put on trial, but certainly most colonial lawyers were not going to defend them. Adams did. He not only defended them, but he got them off! The colonists were furious! It was one thing to stand up for justice and honor. That, after all, could be considered noble! But it was quite another

British troops are shown here firing into a crowd of protesting Bostonians on March 5, 1770. The patriot in the center may be Crispus Attucks, a freed black man who was the first colonist killed in the cause of American independence.

matter actually to set the soldiers free! A disgusted Adams returned to Braintree to forget the whole thing.

A few years later he was back in the spotlight, however, egged on by his cousin, Samuel Adams, an ardent patriot who called for action against British colonial policies in America. John began to lend his voice to the growing cries of anti-British protest. In Massachusetts, this led to the Boston Tea Party, which Adams called "magnificent." On December 16, 1773, colonists disguised as Native Americans dumped tea overboard from British ships in Boston Harbor to protest the tax on this product. When the British closed the harbor as punishment, the colonists convened the First Continental Congress in Philadelphia in September 1774. As a delegate, Adams spoke well for the patriot cause. The quiet man returned to Massachusetts as a hero.

By the time of the American Revolution, Adams was past 40 years old and plump. Thinking himself unfit for military service, he became a diplomat, first in France and after the war, in London. When Washington was elected as the nation's first leader, Adams accepted the second spot only because he very much wanted to be President one day himself. He spent a good deal of his vice presidential years worrying about petty details, which drove everyone about him to distraction. Should he follow the President's lead or be his own man? Should he sit down or stand up when talking to Congress? Senator William Maclay of Pennsylvania wrote in his journal, "Who cares?" Adams also had a big worry about official titles. He thought a government couldn't get along without them. In a pointed dig at his weight, someone suggested a title for Adams himself: His Rotundity.

Adams grew to hate the office of vice president, mostly because he had nothing much to do. That complaint is still heard today. In fact, he wrote to his wife that his office was the "most insignificant" ever invented. But finally, it was time for John Adams, at age 61, to become the nation's second President, which he did in 1797.

Like Washington, Adams was a Federalist. He believed in a strong federal government. The U.S. Constitution makes no mention of political parties, but by the election of 1796, the first signs of such organizations were beginning to appear. Adams and Thomas Pinckney were the leading Federalists, and Thomas Jefferson and Aaron Burr were favored by the so-called Democratic-Republicans. The voting ballot did not actually name who was running for what office, such as Adams for President, Pinckney for vice president. Instead, as during Washington's terms, the two highest vote-getters got the jobs. In that way, Adams became President because he had the highest number of electoral votes—71. But Jefferson had only three less, or 68. Therefore, Jefferson, not Pinckney, unexpectedly became vice president. This meant that the country would be led by two men of different political viewpoints.

Adams the intellectual finally had the job he wanted and for which he felt totally qualified. But it only made him more cranky. In the first place, beloved George Washington was a tough act to follow. In the second place, Adams's own vice president, who should have been a great help to him, was head of the opposition! It was a strange way to run a government. In the third place, independent Adams sometimes went his own way and did not always vote with the Federalists. This angered influential Alexander Hamilton. And in the fourth place, Adams's mind and heart were often in Braintree where his beloved Abigail lay ill.

Abigail Smith Adams

To his credit, Adams tried. He tried to patch things up with Hamilton, who was by then practicing law in New York. Even out of government, Hamilton had great influence over the President's Cabinet. But Hamilton would not budge. As far as he was concerned, Adams was betraying Federalist principles, and that was that. In the end, this conflict between the two would ruin the political future of the President and eventually wreck the Federalist Party itself.

Adams tried to make peace with Jefferson, too. This was not easy considering that Jefferson said of the President: "He is vain, irritable, and accurate in his judgment except when knowledge of the world is necessary...." But Adams and Jefferson, two patriots passionate in their love for their young country and desperate to make it work, could not and would not see eye to eye. By the end of Adams's term in office, these two enlightened and intellectual adults were not even speaking to one another.

One principal issue marked and changed the four years of John Adams's presidency and the course of the country. He had to spend nearly all his years in office trying to avoid entanglement in the endless warring between Great Britain and France.

The French, still fighting with the British, were angry when Adams took office in 1797. They were angry about Jay's Treaty because they felt that the United States, which claimed to be neutral, had given in to England. They were angry because they believed, correctly, that most Federalists favored the British. Adams, however, favored no one and just wanted to avoid war.

Soon, France began to attack American shipping. The French government announced that any American sailors caught on British ships would be treated as pirates!

Adams quickly sent General Charles Cotesworth Pinckney, brother of Thomas, who had run for election with Adams in 1796, to Paris. French foreign minister Talleyrand would not even see him! This was most embarrassing. Federalists, urged on by Hamilton, called for war.

President Adams thought better of it. Instead, he sent Pinckney and two other ministers, John Marshall and Ellsworth Gerry, back to Paris. In secret, Talleyrand sent three agents of his own to meet them. The agents whispered that France would agree to U.S. proposals *if* President Adams would make a public apology for speaking badly of the earlier French Revolution and *if* the U.S. government would make a large cash settlement on the Directory, which ran the French government.

Declared the insulted foreign minister Pinckney, "No, no, not a sixpence!" Vowed the insulted President Adams, "I will make this public!" And he did. But in his report to the American people in April 1798, Adams substituted the letters X, Y, and Z for the actual names of the secret French agents. That is how this almost-war incident came to be known as the "X,Y,Z Affair."

The reaction was immediate and emotional. After returning from France some months later, John Marshall spoke at a dinner. He changed Pinckney's rather mild reply to the French insult into the far more dramatic, and often quoted, "Millions for defense, but not one cent for tribute!" Federalists demanded war! Jefferson, minister to France in the 1780s and decidedly pro-French, and his party demanded to see proof that the President was telling the truth about this whole affair! He was, and even Jefferson had to agree with Adams.

Trade with France was suspended, a navy department was established, and the hero of the Revolution, General George Washington himself, was called out of retirement. Washington had agreed only after Adams promised to make Hamilton a general and Washington's second in command.

Some fighting did take place on the high seas between the two countries over the next two years. But actual war was never declared. France was

The U.S.S. Constellation *and* L'Insurgente, *a French ship, in combat, February 9, 1799, during the undeclared war between the two countries.*

embarrassed by the whole affair. Talleyrand seemed a bit stunned himself. He had not meant to start an armed conflict! He told Adams, through the President's son, John Quincy Adams, that any American minister to Paris would now be received with proper respect. The Treaty of Morfontaine was signed on September 30, 1800, restoring good relations between France and the United States and ending the X,Y,Z Affair.

But it didn't end the President's problems. He was still caught in the middle. The Federalists were furious because he had backed down and not gone to war. The Republicans were furious because Congress had passed all sorts of military bills and panicked the public—all for what? they said. As for John Adams, he just did what he thought was right for the country.

There was still one last bit of controversy for President Adams. It took the form of the Alien and Sedition Acts, passed by Congress in mid-1798. One, the Naturalization Act, increased from 5 to 15 the number of years a foreigner must live in the United States before becoming a citizen. Two alien acts (Alien Act and Alien Enemies Act) allowed the President to expel aliens in peace or war if they were thought to be a threat to national security. The Sedition Act, the most controversial of the acts, made it illegal to conspire against or to publish or even speak any false or malicious criticism of the government. The Federalists in Congress passed the acts to silence any opponents, despite the objection of Adams and others. The Republicans said the acts violated the First Amendment. Adams, once more the middleman, signed the acts and then ignored them, thereby pleasing neither side. At any rate, there was little enforcement. However, a man in Newark, New Jersey, did receive a fine of $100 because he said out loud that he wished a wad from a cannon would lodge itself in the President's backside! The acts all expired or were repealed by 1800.

Before the election of 1800, on November 1 of that year, John Adams arrived in Washington, D.C., from Philadelphia, to

The White House, seen from the garden, as it might have appeared in 1799.

become the nation's first President to sleep in the White House. Although he stayed there alone because Abigail was still in Massachusetts, the mansion was now officially the home of the Presidents. Wrote the President to his wife on his second day in the White House:

> *I Pray Heaven to Bestow The Best of Blessings*
> *on THIS HOUSE and on All that shall hereafter*
> *Inhabit it. May none but Honest and Wise Men*
> *ever rule under This Roof.*

Later, President Franklin D. Roosevelt had those words cut into the mantel in the White House for all to see.

It is a glorious tribute to the nation, this home of Presidents. On 18 acres with more than 130 rooms, it sits on a hillside that slopes down to the Potomac River on the south. The exterior is arkose sandstone from the Aquia Creek quarry in Virginia. The basement walls are 13 feet high and 3 feet thick. The beautifully decorated interior is a treasure of artworks and furniture that tell the splendid history of America. From its original cost of about $300,000, the White House was completely renovated during the administration of Harry S Truman, in 1952, at a cost of nearly $6 million.

The White House today is a true national treasure, but to its first occupants it probably did not look like much. In fact, when Abigail Adams arrived, two weeks after the President moved in, she was appalled! And well she should have been, for the building wasn't even finished. Half of the 36 rooms hadn't been plastered. There was no running water, of course, so that had to be carried from half a mile away. The front yard was muddy and full of junk. To get to the front door, one had to walk across a wooden plank. Bathroom facilities were in the backyard. Said Mrs. Adams in a letter to her daughter, "This is a great drafty castle." It was also cold the First Lady complained, because she couldn't find enough people to chop wood and cart it into the house.

The first term of John Adams had only four months to go. And despite the stormy years, he very much wanted a second term. Yet, he had to wait until December for the Electoral College, which elected the President, to meet. Although presidential elections were held in November just as they are today, the new President did not take office until the following March. Communication and travel time were much slower then. Since John and Abigail Adams did not yet know if he would have a second term, the First Lady, being a practical woman, did little work on the White House decorations for the time being. She hung a Gilbert Stuart portrait of George Washington on a wall and strung up a clothesline in the huge East Room (now the site of elegant receptions). Then John and Abigail Adams waited.

Adams lost the election of 1800. It did not help him that his bitter feud with Hamilton had weakened the Federalists.

Americans were also furious about the Alien and Sedition Acts. The defeat of John Adams marked the end of the Federalists as a major political force.

Adams was bitterly disappointed by the loss. After he thought about it, however, he told his wife that his defeat was probably good for the country because he was going to die soon anyway. Abigail just smiled and packed up the clothesline.

The former President did not even stay in Washington long enough for the inauguration of his old rival, Thomas Jefferson. Instead, he and Abigail returned to the house in Quincy, today a national historic site, where they shared many happy years with their family. Adams busied himself with farming, correspondence, and keeping his journals. Abigail died of typhoid in 1818 and so could not share her husband's joy when their oldest son, John Quincy, became President of the United States in 1825.

John Adams was a difficult man to be sure. But this young country, to which he was so totally devoted, was fortunate to have him follow Washington. Adams was wise and honest to a fault, with the courage to stand up for what he believed was right. Like all these Presidents of the early years and perhaps more than at any other time, Adams put country first in all his actions. He passed on to the next administration a young, weak, and still unsure nation, but one firmly on the path to sound government and principles of honor. That is perhaps his greatest contribution. Like Washington before him and Jefferson after him, John Adams was indeed a patriot.

Ironically, Adams's defeat did not write the final chapter in his dealings with Jefferson. After years of bitter silence between them, in 1812 Adams sent a letter to Monticello, to which Jefferson had retired three years earlier. A warm and flourishing correspondence began between the two old patriots, filled with ideas about current affairs and fond remembrances of the country's birth.

To prove once again that truth is indeed stranger than fiction, 90-year-old John Adams, as he lay dying, spoke these last words: "Jefferson still survives." In fact, however, Adams was wrong. Thomas Jefferson had died just a few hours earlier at Monticello. These two heroes of the Revolution and Presidents of the young republic had both died on the Fourth of July, 1826, exactly 50 years after the Declaration of Independence.

Names in the News in Adams's Time

Samuel Adams (1722–1803):

Radical leader in the Massachusetts colony who inspired the Boston Tea Party. He prodded his shy cousin, John Adams, into patriot action.

John Hancock (1737–1793):

Massachusetts patriot who became a popular hero when charged by the British with smuggling wine into Boston (1768). Defended by John Adams; case withdrawn by the British. Because of his "large" penmanship when he signed the Declaration of Independence, his name has come to mean the same as "signature."

Charles Cotesworth Pinckney (1746–1825):

Revolutionary general, statesman from South Carolina. Adams's minister to France during the X,Y,Z Affair.

Thomas Pinckney (1750–1828):

Brother of Charles, governor of South Carolina (1787–1789), Federalist candidate with John Adams (1796), congressman (1797–1801).

Chapter Three

The Remarkable Skills of Thomas Jefferson

Thomas Jefferson (1801-1809)

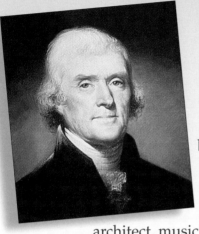

*W*hat to call the man who became the third President of the United States? Was he a statesman and politician? Of course. Was he a lawyer, farmer, architect, musician, philosopher, and writer? Yes. Was he a geographer, scientist, surveyor, naturalist, botanist, and linguist? Indeed, he was. He also read classical literature and studied fossils. These were not idle interests for Jefferson. He actually read Latin, Greek, French, and Spanish. He invented a plow to aid farming, and he mastered the violin. He compiled a vocabulary of Native American languages. He kept records of tree and flower growth and the migrations of birds. He once smuggled an unusual variety of rice across the Italian border to take home to America.

In addition, during his lifetime, Thomas Jefferson was minister to France, governor of Virginia, secretary of state, vice president, and the third President of the United States for two terms. For all that, the accomplishment that gave him the most pride was the founding of the University of Virginia. Indeed, Thomas Jefferson was a remarkable man.

Of course, not everyone thought so. As we know, there was little love lost between Jefferson and John Adams until their later years. Adams must have been feeling really angry in 1797, for he said, "...I am obliged to look upon Jefferson as a man whose mind is warped by prejudice and so blinded by ignorance as to be unfit for the office he holds." Remember that at the time, Jefferson was Adams's own vice president! John Randolph of Roanoke, Virginia, in Congress during the Jefferson administration, apparently not only disliked his President but the whole nation as well. Randolph said, "I cannot live in this miserable, undone country," adding sarcastically that he had never seen so many pilgrims at a shrine as attend the "saint of Monticello," meaning Jefferson. And Alexander Hamilton was convinced that under his polished manners, Jefferson had a mad thirst for power. More charitable colleagues just said he was cold, cynical, and bitter!

This man of remarkable skills was born on April 13, 1743, on the western frontier of the Virginia colony. He was one of ten children. His father, Peter Jefferson, was a well-to-do tobacco plantation owner. His mother, Jane Randolph Jefferson, came from one of Virginia's "first" families. The Jefferson family home, in what is now Albemarle County, was called Shadwell.

Young Thomas was educated by a tutor and then, after his father's death in 1757, in a log cabin classroom. At the age of 17 he attended the College of William and Mary in Williamsburg, the capital of the colony. Founded in 1693, William and Mary is the second oldest college in the United States, after Harvard.

By the time Jefferson graduated, in 1762, he was well over six feet tall, gangly, freckle-faced, and redheaded. He showed a brilliant mind but was inclined to be somewhat lazy. After a few years in the Williamsburg law offices of George Wythe, Jefferson passed the bar exam in 1767.

In 1772, he married a beautiful young widow, Martha Wayles Skelton. They moved into the still unfinished Monticello, which means "little mountain," in central Virginia. It became Jefferson's beloved lifelong home and is now a national historic landmark. Of their six children, only Martha, called Patsy, and Maria, called Polly, lived to adulthood. For many years, his wife was in

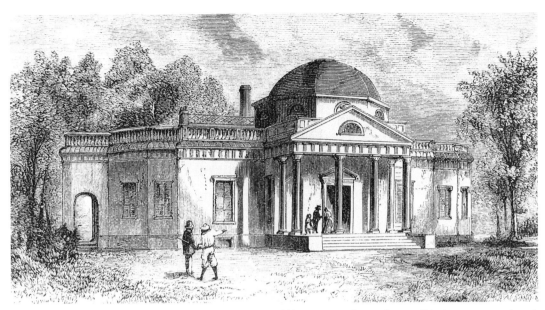

Monticello, Jefferson's home in central Virginia, is shown here after it was completed.

fragile health and she died in 1782 at the early age of 33. Jefferson never remarried.

For all his service to the United States, arguably Jefferson's most glorious contribution occurred before he lived in the White House. As war with Great Britain drew near, the colonists convened the Continental Congress in Philadelphia. In June 1776, Richard Henry Lee of Virginia proposed that "these United Colonies are and of right ought to be free and independent states...." The Congress appointed a committee of five, among them Thomas Jefferson, to draft a formal resolution to that effect. The committee, including John Adams and Benjamin Franklin, gave the writing job to Jefferson. The committee made few changes to the work that Jefferson took about one week to compose. His magnificent ode to freedom and one of the most important of all American historical documents begins, "When in the course of human events, it becomes necessary for one people to dissolve the political bands which have connected them with another..." It ends, "And for the support of this

The committee assigned to draft the Declaration of Independence consisted of (left to right) Benjamin Franklin (Pennsylvania), Thomas Jefferson (Virginia), Robert R. Livingston (New York), John Adams (Massachusetts), and Roger Sherman (Connecticut).

Declaration, with a firm reliance on the protection of Divine Providence, we mutually pledge to each other our Lives, our Fortunes and our sacred Honor." Announced on July 4, 1776, it is known to Americans and to the world as the Declaration of Independence.

Jefferson was the governor of Virginia during the American Revolution. He was criticized in that post for his failure to cooperate with the Virginia legislature. At war's end, he was a member of the Continental Congress, 1783–1784. He is responsible for naming the dollar as the national unit of currency. He also worked to establish the government of what became the Northwest Territory. From 1785 to 1789, he was minister to France and so was out of the country during the drafting of the U.S. Constitution. He received a copy of it when in Paris and urged the inclusion of a bill of rights. Jefferson returned home to become Washington's secretary of state in 1789 and then, unwillingly, became vice president under John Adams in 1797.

In the election of 1800, Federalists Adams and Charles C. Pinckney were opposed by the Democratic-Republican ticket of Jefferson and Aaron Burr. A former senator from New York,

Burr (1756–1836) was a brilliant but egotistical political leader. The Democratic-Republicans won, but Jefferson and Burr each had 73 electoral votes. Although everyone knew that Jefferson was running for President and Burr for vice president, the election ballots didn't say so. Therefore, when they ended up with the same number of electoral votes, each had won a tie for the presidency!

This threw the choice of President into the House of Representatives to break the tie. The House voted 35 times by state. It was still a tie. Finally, on the thirty-sixth ballot, in another stranger-than-fiction episode, the tie was broken in Jefferson's favor by none other than his old enemy Alexander Hamilton! Why? The answer was simple. Hamilton thought that Burr would make a worse President even than Jefferson!

In fact, the hatred between Hamilton and Burr, both living in New York, became so extreme that they ended up in a duel. Burr challenged Hamilton after hearing of some unflattering remarks Hamilton had written about him in a letter. The duel was held on

A wounded Alexander Hamilton is shown being tended by his seconds after his duel with Aaron Burr.

the morning of July 11, 1804, in Weehawken, New Jersey, where dueling was still legal. Hamilton was fatally wounded and died the next day. Burr was later charged with treason for a scheme that involved breaking off the western part of the United States into a separate country and perhaps conquering Mexico. He was acquitted for lack of witnesses and died in New York in 1836, a lonely and forgotten man. According to the story, the only person Burr had ever cared about was his daughter, Theodosia, who lived in the South. When he was quite old, she took a ship north to visit him, but the vessel was apparently lost at sea. It is said that Burr often could be seen walking the New York shores waiting in vain for his daughter's ship.

Jefferson became the third President of the United States in 1800, but the close election had finally sent a wake-up call to Congress. The Twelfth Amendment was passed in 1804. It said that electors must write down two names on the ballot, one person for President and another person for vice president and that the two would not be from the same state.

Jefferson, age 57, became the first President inaugurated in the capital city of Washington, D.C. Conscious of the terrible bitterness left from the election, he tried to set a tone of peace in his inaugural speech. Copies of the speech had to be handed out afterward, however, because Jefferson delivered it in such a quiet voice that only the people standing closest to him heard it at all!

The third President was the first to spend his full administration in the White House—which, incidentally, was still unfinished. Abigail Adams's clothesline was gone from the East Room, but visitors continued to march across a wooden plank to get to the front door, and to make matters worse, the roof leaked. Since no one took care of the grounds, a visitor at night was just as apt to fall into a pit as make it to the front door. Jefferson was not much for ceremony anyhow and mainly lived in one corner of the mansion. In fact, for one so accomplished, he was said to be somewhat sloppy. More than one visitor mistook him for a servant. He was given to wearing old slippers around the White House and sometimes cracked nuts while conducting official business. He was so casual about state dinners that he just let people sit where they wished to and sometimes served the plates himself from the dumbwaiter. These homespun mannerisms highly irritated official ministers from Great Britain and France, who were used to much fuss over their rank.

But even the casual President on occasion had to be a little more formal, if only to honor the country. Because he was a widower, Dolley Madison, wife of James who would succeed Jefferson as President, sometimes acted as White House hostess. In addition, Jefferson's daughters, now married, often visited and acted in that capacity. On one visit in 1805, daughter Patsy gave birth to her eighth child, making James Madison Randolph the first baby to be born in the White House.

Not long after he was sworn in, Jefferson faced his first major crisis in the form of the Barbary pirates. Like the big European powers, the United States under Washington and Adams paid tribute to the so-called Barbary pirates off the shores of Algiers, Tunis, Tripoli, and Morocco on the north African coast. It was easier and cheaper to pay than to fight. In exchange for a high

Commodore Edward Preble's American fleet attacked Tripoli on August 3, 1804, but until 1815 Barbary pirates kept demanding money not to attack American shipping.

ransom, the pirates did not attack American trading ships in the Mediterranean. The very idea of paying tribute infuriated Jefferson. So, when the pasha, Tripoli's leader, embarrassed an American ship's officer in public and then demanded more money, Jefferson said no. The pasha was amused by such an unexpected show of resistance. He retaliated in May 1801 by chopping down the U.S. flagpole in front of the American consulate in Tripoli. In reply, Jefferson sent United States Navy ships to the Mediterranean.

It was a brave show and the American Navy did have some success, but it was not yet strong enough to back up the nation's demands. The Barbary pirates continued to call for, and receive, money until 1815. This crisis in the Mediterranean is remembered in the famous battle song of the United States Marine Corps: "From the halls of Montezuma, to the shores of Tripoli."

Another major crisis of the Jefferson administration and one that still affects every American citizen involved the Supreme Court. When Jefferson took office, it was not clear that the Court had the right to decide whether a law could be declared unconstitutional. Then came the case of *Marbury v. Madison*.

At the end of Adams's term, the Federalist Congress passed the Judiciary Act of 1801. It created a lot of new judgeships. The night before he left office, on March 2, 1801, Adams filled those positions with, of course, Federalists. This was much in the manner of modern-day Presidents who try to appoint people of their own party or beliefs to the Supreme Court and to local courts as well. These new Adams appointees were dubbed "midnight judges." One of them, William Marbury, was appointed to serve as justice of the peace in Washington, D.C.

A problem occurred because, when Jefferson took office the next day, Marbury did not actually have in his hand his signed official appointment. These appointments were hand delivered by the secretary of state. Since the appointment had not been delivered before Jefferson took office, the new President saw a chance to give the position to someone of his own party. He said the appointment of Marbury, granted by Adams, was not legal. Marbury petitioned the Supreme Court to order the new secretary of state, James Madison, to deliver the appointment.

John Marshall of Virginia was the Chief Justice, appointed by Adams. He was a tried-and-true Federalist and, therefore, loathed by Jefferson. If Marshall ordered Madison to issue the appointment, Jefferson might tell Madison not to do so. What could the Court do then? If Marshall refused to give the order to Madison, he would be admitting that the Court could not challenge the President of the United States. It was a prickly decision to make.

But John Marshall was a brilliant man. First, he declared that, despite what the President said, Marbury had a right to his commission. However, said Marshall, it was unconstitutional to *order* Madison to deliver said commission! So, Marbury did not get his judgeship, and it looked as though Jefferson had won. However, what Marshall really did was to establish the right of the Supreme Court to decide what laws are constitutional. This is called "judicial review." That is a power not granted by the U.S. Constitution, and it greatly enhanced the power of the Supreme Court. So it continues to this day.

By far, the most outstanding event of Jefferson's years in the White House was the Louisiana Purchase of 1803. It really made an impact on the United States because it doubled the size of the country. For $15 million, the young nation got another 828,000 square miles of land. That came to three cents an acre, undeniably the best land bargain in U.S. history!

When Jefferson took office in 1801, the United States was made up of 16 states: the original 13 colonies, plus Vermont (1791), Kentucky (1792), and Tennessee (1796). In addition, the United States claimed territory from western Pennsylvania to the Mississippi River, north to Canada, and south to portions of what are now Alabama and Mississippi. With the Louisiana

Purchase, the United States added the territory west of the Mississippi River to the Rocky Mountains, north to Canada, and south to the Gulf of Mexico. It came about in this way...

In 1803, France owned the Louisiana Territory as well as the Port of New Orleans on the Gulf of Mexico, at the mouth of the Mississippi River. Jefferson dreamed of expanding the country to the west. This concept that it was the right, and even the duty, of the United States to expand its territory and influence in North America was known as Manifest Destiny. Jefferson knew that was impossible without American control of shipping on the river and through the port. With the approval of Congress, Jefferson instructed his minister to France, Robert R. Livingston, to offer the French emperor, Napoleon, $2 million for New Orleans. To Livingston's—and Jefferson's—surprise, Napoleon said, "Why just one city? Why not the whole territory?"

Why, indeed? Why such an offer? For one reason, France was short of money. For another, Emperor Napoleon's plans for a French empire in the New World had gone sour. A few

The Louisiana Purchase ceremony took place in New Orleans December 20, 1803, on the occasion of the treaty's signature.

years earlier his troops were badly defeated when they tried to reconquer the Caribbean island of Santo Domingo, which today is divided into Haiti and the Dominican Republic. The third reason was Great Britain. Napoleon the general knew that if he tried to expand in the New World, eventually he would have to fight the British. He also knew his country was no match for the mighty Royal Navy. It was more desirable to sell the land to the Americans than lose it to the British.

Surprised and delighted at Napoleon's offer, Jefferson instructed Livingston to buy the Louisiana Territory for a total of $15 million. And he did. In actual fact, Jefferson did not have the power to make the purchase. The U.S. Congress had authorized only $2 million. The Constitution did not say anything about acquiring new land, and Jefferson knew that by the time an amendment could be passed, the deal would be lost. So, he chose to stretch the Constitution and present the purchase to Congress as a deal completed. The pro-Jefferson Congress agreed. The treaty was signed on October 20, 1803. The following year Jefferson sent Meriwether Lewis and William Clark to map the Missouri River and explore the newly acquired land in the west. The expansion of America to the Pacific was on.

Sacagawea, a Native American guide, showed explorers Lewis and Clark the way through the Rocky Mountains in 1805.

By election time 1804, Jefferson was riding high. Americans were pleased with the Louisiana Purchase. They rather liked their tall, gangly President even if he did wear darned socks and serve French food at the White House. Against the Federalists, he easily won reelection—162 to 14 for opponent Charles Cotesworth Pinckney—along with Vice President George Clinton, former New York governor. Clinton had replaced Aaron Burr after the duel that killed Hamilton.

Perhaps Jefferson should have quit while he was ahead. His second term soon began to slide downhill. In 1806, the endless fighting between England and France once again created problems in the New World. American ships and sailors were seized and harrassed. President Jefferson tried the Embargo Act. He simply stopped all U.S. exports to both countries.

The Embargo Act did not greatly damage France or England, but it nearly caused a civil war at home. And it brought Jefferson's popularity crashing down on his head. Farm prices fell. Goods rotted on the wharves. Ships rotted at the docks. Manufacturers in New England talked about getting out of the Union! Smuggling into British Canada made a mockery of the law anyway. Finally, Jefferson had to give in. He asked Congress to lift the embargo, which was done by mid-June 1809 after Jefferson had left office.

Another problem in his second term concerned former Vice President Aaron Burr. After involving himself in a shady scheme about western lands and concerning Mexico, Burr was tried for

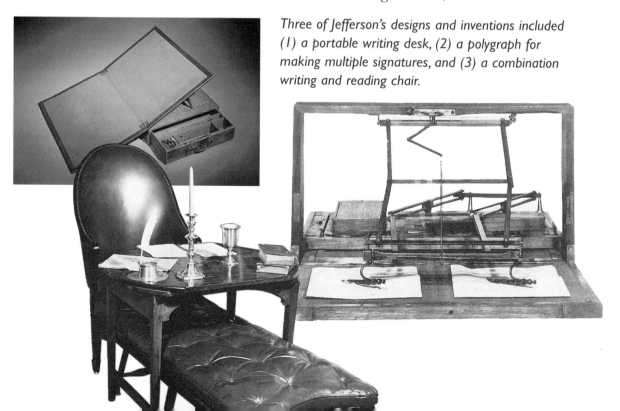

Three of Jefferson's designs and inventions included (1) a portable writing desk, (2) a polygraph for making multiple signatures, and (3) a combination writing and reading chair.

treason and acquitted. But before Chief Justice John Marshall announced the verdict, Jefferson said that Burr should be found guilty. This seemed odd conduct from the man who had supported the Bill of Rights guaranteeing every American a fair jury trial. Yet, in this episode, as always, Jefferson's primary concern was the welfare and security of his country.

Although some urged Jefferson to seek a third term, he had had enough of this "splendid misery" and retired at age 66 to his beloved Monticello. There he resumed his activities as farmer, inventor, botanist, writer, philosopher, and spoiler of grandchildren. He corresponded with former foe John Adams and, with great pride and delight, designed the buildings for the University of Virginia (1819) at Charlottesville. He personally supervised its construction, chose its faculty, and selected the books for its library.

On July 4, 1826, the third President of the United States died a few hours before the second President. He had been near death on the 3rd, but woke from a delirium to ask the date. It seemed as though he was determined to live until the fiftieth anniversary of his most splendid document, the Declaration of Independence.

Thomas Jefferson had his detractors and his faults. For instance, although he was a champion of freedom and individual rights, he was also a slaveowner, like many men of his class, times, and location. He freed only five slaves during his lifetime and most of them in his will. However, even that was more than most slaveowners did. When the issue of slavery came up, he avoided a stand. He saw the evils of slavery but saw slavery as a necessary evil. And during his second term, he made some poor decisions, such as supporting the Embargo Act.

It could be said, however, that the Declaration of Independence and the Louisiana Purchase were enough to change the destiny of his country and mark Jefferson as one of its greatest statesmen. But there was more to this President. Perhaps one of his greatest contributions was his firm belief in the separation of church and state. He chose these words to be engraved on his tombstone: "Here was buried Thomas Jefferson, author of the Declaration of American Independence, of the statute of Virginia for religious freedom, and father of the University of Virginia."

Jefferson believed that indeed "all men are created equal" under the law, just as he believed that this young nation would become the world's great example of liberty. He was not a flawless leader, nor was he "the saint of Monticello." But Thomas Jefferson, third President of the United States, was, indeed, a most remarkable man.

Names in the News in Jefferson's Time

Richard Henry Lee (1732–1794):

Aristocratic statesman who declared in the Continental Congress of 1776 that "these united colonies are, and of right ought to be, free and independent states," a statement leading to the Declaration of Independence and the American Revolution. One of the Lee family of Virginia, whose members included Revolutionary hero Henry "Lighthorse Harry" (1756–1818) and his son, Robert E. (1807–1870), Commander in Chief of the Confederate armies in the Civil War.

Meriwether Lewis (1774–1809):

American explorer, private secretary to Jefferson; with William Clark (1770–1838) explored Louisiana Purchase. They sailed up the Missouri River, crossed the Continental Divide, and navigated the Columbia River to the Pacific Ocean (1804–1806). One of their guides was Sacagawea (c.1787–1812), a Native American woman of the Shoshone people.

Robert R. Livingston (1746–1813):

Born in New York City, member of the Continental Congress, one of committee of five, along with Jefferson, that drew up the Declaration of Independence. Gave oath of office to George Washington, New York City, April 30, 1789.

John Marshall (1755–1835):

Virginia-born lawyer who served as Chief Justice of the Supreme Court (1801–1835). Staunch Federalist and distant cousin of Thomas Jefferson, who loathed him. With his decision on *Marbury v. Madison*, he gave the Supreme Court its greatest power, that of deciding on the constitutionality of laws.

Meriwether Lewis is portrayed dressed in furs that he might have worn on the expedition to the Pacific.

Chapter Four

The Friendly Home of James and Dolley Madison

James Madison (1809-1817)

*I*f, as the saying goes, "good things come in small packages," then, James Madison was the best. He was the shortest of all U.S. Presidents— five feet six, and he weighed barely 100 pounds. Sickly, bookish, and a poor speaker, he was also witty, learned, and as the father of the U.S. Constitution, a giant in his country's history.

The third Virginian to become President, Madison was born at Port Conway on March 16, 1751. His father's plantation was on the edge of the wild Appalachian Mountains. Most of his playmates were the children of the plantation's slaves. Madison grew up a staunch foe of slavery.

In his early years, his mother taught him to read and write. When he was 18, in 1769, he went north to the College of New Jersey (now Princeton University). This was most unusual. Wealthy Virginians of the day sent their sons to be educated at the College of William and Mary in Williamsburg, or perhaps abroad—certainly not to another, meaning inferior, colony. But the college in New Jersey attracted students from all the colonies, and it taught tolerance of all religions, which is exactly what the elder Madison had in mind.

Young James thought about becoming a minister after he graduated in 1771, but his poor health put off a decision on his future. The American Revolution resolved that problem. Because he thought he could best serve his country politically,

James Madison, a delegate from Virginia to the Constitutional Convention in Philadelphia in 1787, is seated at the far end of the first row to the left of the three standing delegates.

Madison was active in Virginia's government throughout the war.

James Madison was one of 55 delegates to the Constitutional Convention in Philadelphia in 1787. In four months, from May to September, these men created the remarkable document that sets the United States of America apart from all nations. Many of these delegates were among the most qualified people America had for the job. Most were college educated, unusual for the day. Most were lawyers. Only William Few of Georgia was a working farmer. Most had been active in and were knowledgeable about colonial governments. Among them were Washington, Hamilton, and Benjamin Franklin, who was then 81 years old. The two prominent names missing from the convention were John Adams, then minister to Great Britain, and Thomas Jefferson, then minister to France.

Madison's Virginia Plan, which was presented at the convention and became the basis of the U.S. Constitution, called for three branches of government: the executive (the President), the legislative (Congress), and the judicial (the Supreme Court).

Representatives to the two houses of Congress would be based on state population. That naturally favored the larger states. And that naturally brought a loud protest from the smaller states. They wanted the New Jersey plan: one state, one vote. The convention ground to a halt. Finally, Franklin offered a compromise. Congress would have two houses, called a bicameral legislature, as Madison suggested. One house would be based on population (the House) and the other on one state, one vote—actually one state, two votes (the Senate). Madison agreed to the compromise and urged the delegates to do likewise.

That problem was barely over when another one emerged. If the number of delegates to the House of Representatives were to be based on total population, what about slaves? The slave states of the South naturally wanted them counted as part of the total number. Northern states of course did not. Although Madison detested slavery and wanted it abolished altogether, he realized that without compromise, the southern states would not vote for the Constitution. So, he suggested that five slaves be counted as three free men. It was a compromise he disliked but one he felt was necessary to create the government.

The Constitution of the United States was approved by the delegates on September 17, 1787. Now began the process of getting the states to ratify, or approve, it. Toward that end, Madison joined Alexander Hamilton and John Jay in writing the so-called Federalist Papers. Later collected in book form under the title *The Federalist*, they remain, to this day, the greatest original work in the field of U.S. government.

Delaware was the first state to ratify the Constitution, on December 7, but nine states had to agree before it became the law of the land. That happened when New Hampshire approved it on June 21, 1788. Days later, Virginia followed. Since word had not yet reached the South that the Constitution already had the required number of votes for ratification, for a time, Virginia believed that it was the deciding state. Stubborn little Rhode

Island didn't want to approve it at all! It finally did ratify in May 1790, but only after Congress threatened to treat the smallest of the states as a foreign power if it didn't.

Madison was elected to the House of Representatives for four terms and became Jefferson's secretary of state in 1801. With Jefferson's endorsement in the presidential election of 1808, Madison, a Democratic-Republican, defeated Federalist Charles Cotesworth Pinckney of South Carolina, 122–47. Said the third President about the fourth: "I do not know in the world a man of purer integrity...nor could I point out an abler head."

Perhaps so, but scholarly Madison, age 58, did not have the political skills of those who had held the office before him. The administration of this brilliant man was marked by disaster and ended in an unnecessary war.

Madison was sometimes indecisive and often could not or would not stand up to his stronger willed colleagues. For instance, when he took office, he wanted the very able Albert Gallatin, Jefferson's secretary of the treasury, to become secretary of state. But Congress said no, keep him in the Treasury, and the President backed down.

Not all of Madison's problems could be blamed on his lack of aggressiveness, for, in truth, Jefferson had left him with a monumental mess. The problem was how not to get entangled in the constant warfare between France and Great Britain. Jefferson had merely put off the problem, not solved it. That dilemma was dumped on the frail shoulders of the fourth President.

Congress had repealed the disastrous Embargo Act in 1809, only to pass the disastrous Non-Intercourse Act. This said that the United States could trade with anyone—*except* France and Great Britain. By the time Madison took office, on March 1, 1809, this latest restriction was getting on Britain's nerves, to say nothing of getting into British wallets. With France sealing off most European countries, English merchants saw the United States as a very inviting, but forbidden, trade market.

Britain's foreign secretary, George Canning, was lukewarm about America. But under pressure from English businessmen and manufacturers, he told his minister in Washington, D.C., David M. Erskine, to reach an agreement. Erskine responded in a most generous fashion. He was rather fond of Americans, perhaps because he was married to one. He told Madison that Great Britain would stop harassing American ships and sailors and would lift trade restrictions, and the United States did not have to do a thing in return.

Madison was, of course, delighted. He was also hasty. Without waiting for official word from London, he lifted the embargo on U.S. trade with Britain. Immediately, American ships sailed for Great Britain.

This was a wrong move. When the foreign secretary got word of the agreement, he was furious! He recalled affable Erskine and replaced him with Francis James Jackson. To say that Jackson disliked Americans was not the half of it. He called the President "mean looking" and said Mrs. Madison was "fat and forty."

An embarrassed President was forced to restore the embargo. Then, Congress passed Macon's Bill Number 2. It was naively intended to pit France and Britain against each other instead of against the United States. The bill restored U.S. trade with both nations. However, if France restored normal relations with America, then America would stop trading with Britain. And if Britain restored normal relations with America, then, of course, America would stop trading with France.

Another wrong move. Napoleon saw through it immediately. Sending a flowery letter to the President, the emperor declared all French restrictions canceled. President Madison, alas, fell into the trap. When he asked for a similar promise from Great Britain, he was turned down.

It didn't take long after that for the trusting President to realize he had been duped. By December 1810, Napoleon had seized American ships in French ports and raised the tariffs on American goods.

The tug-of-war went on until mid-1812. Unable to budge France, Madison still insisted that Great Britain lift its restrictions against the United States. After refusing for so long, Great Britain was suffering economically and ready for a change of heart. On June 16, 1812, it lifted restrictions on American trade. It was all in vain.

This was not a time of telephone lines and fax machines. The day after Britain lifted trade restrictions, President Madison asked the Congress to declare war. Neither side knew what the other had done until sometime later. In one more stranger than fiction case, war was declared the day after the reason for it was gone.

Officially, it is known as the War of 1812. Some had other names. Those who were for it called it "the second war of American independence." Those who didn't like the President called it "Mr. Madison's War." By whatever name, on paper, it looks like a flimsy excuse for armed fighting. France had treated the United States as badly as Great Britain had. Why pick on the British?

There were a number of reasons. The President seems to have allowed the country to drift into war rather than being decisive about a policy. The country was growing. Before the war, Louisiana became the eighteenth state. The newcomers in Congress, especially from the western and southern states, were tired of what they saw as years of humiliating treatment from Great Britain. These men, mostly young and relatively inexperienced in government, were known as the War Hawks, and they wanted revenge. Also, the United States was going through an economic depression. Farmers and merchants were angry at British restrictions on trade.

Last but not least, those Americans who wanted to expand into the unsettled western territory accused the British of inciting

A prelude to the War of 1812, American troops drive back retreating Native Americans at the Battle of Tippecanoe on November 7, 1811, near present-day Lafayette, Indiana.

the Indians against them. It was certainly true that many settlers were the victims of attacks by Native Americans. However, it is far more likely that most of the fighting was the result of government policy that robbed the Native American peoples of their homes and hunting grounds without thought or compensation. Such animosity was created that it resulted in the terrible and bloody Battle of Tippecanoe on November 7, 1811. William Henry Harrison, then governor of the Indiana Territory and later ninth President of the United States, had asked Madison for permission to attack the Shawnee chief Tecumseh. The chief was inciting the tribes, Harrison said, who were backed by Great Britain. With the President's reluctant go-ahead, Harrison wiped out the Shawnee, and a new cry, more arrogant than before, went up for revenge against the British.

Even with so many Americans screaming for war, it was a foolish commitment on the part of President Madison. Rarely has a country been so little prepared to fight. The national bank, which might have issued war bonds to finance the fighting, had been abolished the year before. When Congress raised taxes for war goods, many people ignored them. Most ridiculous of all, the United States of America was facing the greatest navy in the history of the world, and it was doing so with about 16 ships! The Royal Navy had hundreds. Just five months before declaring war, the U.S. Congress had turned down a request for ten new naval vessels—they would cost too much money.

But the War Hawks weren't interested in the navy. They planned to defeat the British on land. They would do so simply by capturing Canada! This proved to be not an easy task. For one thing, the American Army had only about 35,000 soldiers, and there was no outstanding leader competent to command them. This was also partly the President's fault, for Madison was a poor Commander in Chief. Without military experience himself, he never appointed a strong leader to coordinate forces. In this manner, all sorts of disasters occurred. In the summer of 1812, General William Hull belatedly realized that he had marched into Canada and stationed his men where they could be cut off by the British. He hastily retreated to Detroit, a little too late. In August the British captured him and his men and the city. The following year, Buffalo fell to the British, and the War Hawks suddenly weren't so certain of victory.

Perhaps the United States could not win the war of superior forces, but it certainly could win the war of slogans. Who knows how much these now immortal words contributed to morale and even victory? Of the many famous war quotes, perhaps the most remembered are the words of Captain James Lawrence. Mortally wounded on his vessel the *Chesapeake* on June 1, 1813, he cried out as he was taken below, "Don't give up the ship!" Another hero, Commodore Oliver Hazard Perry, actually won the Battle of Lake Erie against superior odds on September 10, 1813. Forced to leave his battered ship, the *Lawrence*, he boarded the *Niagara* to continue and win the fight. Afterward he sent off this brief message: "We have met the enemy and they are ours."

Bolstered by some surprising American naval victories and the stubbornness of an outclassed American Army, the fighting drifted into the summer of 1814. But that August, it was to come very close to home for James Madison.

The President had won a second term in 1812, with Elbridge Gerry as vice president. His first vice president, George Clinton, was the first to die in office. Madison got a second term even though five of six antiwar New England states voted for the opposition, New York's DeWitt Clinton, nephew to George.

Although Madison's political life was filled with problems and turmoil through the years, his personal life in the White House was filled with warmth and gaiety. In 1794, Madison had married a vivacious widow, Dolley Payne Todd. Their happy marriage seems to have been marred only by Dolley's spoiled and ne'er-do-well son, Payne, whom Madison adopted and loved. James and Dolley Madison brought in the "golden age" of White House entertaining. The charming and friendly Dolley, who had often served as Jefferson's hostess, soon had Washington society clamoring for invitations. With her flowing curls, ostrich feathers stuck in a bright turban, and dramatic gowns of silk and satin, the First Lady was polished, elegant, talkative, and admired. Writer Washington Irving described her as a "fine, portly...dame who has a smile for everybody." Even the bookish President, whom his wife called "little Jemmy," became an animated and witty dinner companion at these lavish functions. The White House shone with new paint and fine decorations, and guests no longer had to fear falling into a pit while trying to enter the front door. In fact, during this period comes the first mention of the White House actually being referred to by that name, in a letter written by a British diplomat. All too soon, this "golden age"—and nearly the White House itself—was to disappear.

Dolley Payne Todd Madison

By the middle of 1814, the French emperor Napoleon had been exiled to the island of Elba. The war between France and England was over. Now the British could turn full attention to the pesky Americans. British troops landed in Maryland and began a march on Washington, D.C. On the oppressively hot morning of August 22, enemy cannon fire was heard in the city. The President rode out astride his horse to within sight of the front line. Dolley was left at home with a spyglass and 100 soldiers to guard her and the White House. Unfortunately, the soldiers soon left to fight the British, leaving only a few guards behind.

The First Lady spent the day alternatively looking for the return of her husband and trying to decide what to take with her if she had to flee. Finally, a note came from the President telling her to leave the White House and meet him in Virginia. In a wagon loaded with what silver she could manage, plus the Gilbert Stuart portrait of Washington, Dolley Madison left the White House for the last time. Washington's portrait, restored and hanging in the White House today, is the only object that has been in the President's home since 1800.

Dolley left none too soon. The British invaded and set fire to the city. Only a rainstorm saved the White House from being burned to the ground, but the building was left a blackened shell. Only the walls remained. The pride of the young country was badly wounded. This was the President's home, a national symbol of strength and liberty. Now it was gone, and the President had been forced to flee before the enemy. It was a very low ebb in America's history.

An English colored engraving (1815) illustrates British soldiers burning Washington, D.C., on August 24, 1814. The White House, the Capitol, and all the department buildings with the exception of the Patent Office were damaged.

The symbol may have been nearly destroyed, but the country was not lost. That September 13, 1814, the British bombarded Fort McHenry in Chesapeake Bay throughout the night. Francis Scott Key was one of those who waited for the morning. When it came, he wrote that "by the dawn's early light...the flag was still there" and gave the country a national anthem. On Christmas Eve, the two nations signed a treaty at Ghent, Belgium. This unfortunate war ended in a strange way. The last battle, when General Andrew Jackson defeated the British at New Orleans on January 8, 1815, was waged when the war was over. Once again, the news had not reached the interested parties on time.

Neither side had won. The United States had gained nothing by the treaty. But at least peace was restored, and the President was a hero in his country's eyes. "Little Jemmy" had stood up to the mighty British.

The White House was rebuilt in three years, more grand than before. However, it was not finished in time for the Madisons to return, and in 1817, they retired to their home in Montpelier, Virginia. Dolley continued to entertain lavishly, and James became a gentleman farmer, later following Jefferson as head of the University of Virginia. He wrote his autobiography and worked for the abolition of slavery. The fourth President died on June 27, 1836, and was buried at Montpelier. A year later, Dolley returned to Washington and the society she loved. Perhaps it is fitting that her last public appearance was at a ball for President James K. Polk in 1848. She died shortly thereafter at the age of 81.

James Madison was not the strongest of leaders. He was at times indecisive and too hasty or too easily led. But no fault of character can detract from his enormous contribution to the establishment of the United States of America. His role at the Constitutional Convention is made all the more remarkable when one considers how deeply Madison believed in and argued for an absolutely strong federal government and how much he detested slavery. Yet, when the convention appeared stalemated over the makeup of Congress and the question of the slave population, it was Madison who was willing to compromise and urged others to do so. More than any other, he saved the convention and earned himself the title of Father of the U.S. Constitution.

Names in the News in Madison's Time

Stephen Decatur (1779–1820):

Naval officer hero in the War of 1812 and instrumental in stopping payment demands from Barbary pirates (1815). Famous for toast: "Our country! ...may she always be in the right; but our country, right or wrong!" Died in a duel.

Albert Gallatin (1761–1849):

Swiss-born secretary of the treasury under Jefferson and Madison, financial genius. Negotiator during peace treaty, War of 1812. Minister to France and Great Britain, president of the National Bank.

Elbridge Thomas Gerry (1744–1814):

Became Madison's vice president after death of George Clinton and the second vice president to die in office. When governor of Massachusetts, set up geographical voting districts in such a way as to favor his party. First such district was shaped like a salamander, a long-bodied, short-legged animal with a long tail. So the practice became known, as it still is today, as "gerrymandering."

Zebulon Montgomery Pike (1779–1813):

New Jersey-born army officer and explorer. Led exploration of Mississippi, Arkansas, and Red Rivers (1805–1807). Discovered Colorado mountain (Pikes Peak) named for him. In War of 1812, commanded troops in successful assault on York (Toronto), Canada, but killed in battle.

Chapter Five

Monroe and the Era of Good Feeling

James Monroe (1817-1825)

*P*arty-loving Washington folk got a shock in 1817 when James and Elizabeth Monroe moved into the White House. The warmth and gaiety of the Madisons were replaced by the cool reserve of the new presidential family.

After the fire of 1814, James Hoban, the original builder, took three years to restore the mansion. The cost was about the same—$300,000. The President's home gleamed with new white paint. Congress approved $50,000 to restore the interior with handsome furniture and elegant art objects. Still, the heart of the house seemed missing.

Gone were the joyous parties and bubbly ways of Dolley Madison. In her place was Elizabeth Kortright Monroe. The new First Lady was regarded as a bit snooty. She would not tolerate visitors just "dropping in," as was the custom. Unlike previous First Ladies, she refused to respond to any and all invitations. Not so much antisocial, but rather aristocratic and reserved befitting a gentlewoman of the time, she felt little in common with the sometimes rough mannered, often unsophisticated Washington society. So, instead of attending dinners or teas, Mrs. Monroe was inclined to send daughter Eliza Hay. This did little to soothe any ruffled feathers. Educated in Paris and friendly with royalty, Eliza had a rather high opinion of herself and was, if possible, more reserved than her mother.

So, the White House became a formal place, by invitation only, with strict rules of proper behavior. This so insulted congressional wives that they simply refused to attend White House functions. Wrote the wife of a Washington newspaper editor, "The drawing-room of the President was opened last night to a row of empty chairs... Only five females attended, and three of them were foreigners."

But after all, the White House *is* the White House. Before long, Washington society either had to accept the reserved ways of the Monroes or be left out. Most of them did not want to be left out. In fact, future First Ladies owed Mrs. Monroe a debt of gratitude. She forever freed them from the custom of formally responding to everyone's invitation.

Elizabeth Kortright Monroe

As the Monroes were opening a new era in the White House, the President himself was closing an old one. The early years of the new nation were coming to an end, as were the formality and fashions of the eighteenth century. Actually, Monroe himself looked a little old-fashioned for the times. His knee-length pantaloons and white-topped boots were already out of style. Monroe somewhat resembled George Washington. He stood tall and a little awkwardly, his steel-gray hair powdered and tied in back, his blue-gray eyes steady and kind.

The fourth Virginian to become President, Monroe looked and acted much like an aristocrat. Actually, his landowning family, from Westmoreland County, was neither rich nor poor. He was the oldest of five children, born on April 28, 1758. As a youngster, he walked to school with his friend John Marshall, who would become Chief Justice of the United States.

There was much talk of government and liberty in the Monroe household. The boy's uncle was a friend to both Washington and Jefferson, and his father fought for colonial rights. True to custom, Monroe was sent to the College of

William and Mary in 1774, at age 16. Few Americans were college educated in the late 1700s, and even those who were did not always receive a good education, at least by modern standards. The top schools, such as William and Mary or Harvard, out of the 30 or so colleges and universities in Monroe's time, based their programs on Greek and Latin classics. Some theology and mathematics were offered and sometimes history as a separate course, as well as economics, political science, German, and French. Courses in the natural and physical sciences were rarely treated in depth. The budgets of all colleges were based primarily on tuition. It was not unusual for the president of a college also to teach classes to cut down on expenses.

It was difficult for young Monroe to keep his mind on his college studies, however, for there was much talk of ongoing problems with Great Britain. The problems escalated into war, and in 1776, Lieutenant Monroe, as a member of the Third Virginia Regiment, found himself in New York under the command of George Washington. Monroe led his troops in the Christmas night battle at Trenton, New Jersey, and was wounded in the shoulder.

The young man recuperated enough to fight again. He returned to Virginia in 1779, a major at the age of 21. For the next three years, Monroe studied law with Jefferson, then governor of Virginia. The two became lifelong friends. Elected to the Continental Congress, Monroe at first opposed ratifying the U.S. Constitution. He thought it gave the federal government too much power. And whenever a question about slavery came up, Monroe was noticeably absent. Like many an American statesman of his time, he sat on the fence about slavery. He personally thought it was wrong and yet saw it as a necessary evil and owned slaves himself.

Monroe entered the U.S. Senate in 1790. Four years later, Washington named him American minister to France. His first experience as a diplomat got him into trouble with the President.

In 1794, France and Great Britain were at war and relations between the United States and both countries were shaky. France became more upset when Chief Justice John Jay went to London to negotiate a treaty. The French did not want the Americans to side with Britain. So, to smooth things over, Washington sent Monroe to Paris. He was, like Jefferson, a Democratic-Republican, and presumably the French would find him an agreeable envoy. In his first speech in Paris, Monroe assured France that nothing would weaken American-French relationships.

His remarks while in Paris were apparently a little too pro-French and did not sit well with Great Britain. Washington himself thought his diplomat's remarks had gone too far. Saying they were not "well devised," he recalled Monroe in December 1796. Monroe was angry and wrote an attack against the President. Washington, who believed it was the duty of any representative to defend the home country's policy, never forgave him. The two men were never friends again.

Monroe went on other and smoother diplomatic missions. He was also governor of Virginia from 1799 to 1802. Monroe made friends easily. People just naturally liked him. Jefferson said Monroe's "soul might be turned wrong side outwards without discovering a blemish to the world." John C. Calhoun, later Monroe's secretary of war, said that few men were his equal "in wisdom, firmness, and devotion to the country."

Besides having a pleasing personality, Monroe was a very competent administrator. As Madison's secretary of state (1811–1817), he changed a hopelessly muddled department into a smoothly running operation. He did the same for the War Department in 1814 and 1815, while still performing his duties as secretary of state. So, in terms of service to his country, Monroe seemed a logical candidate for the Democratic-Republicans in 1816. He easily beat Rufus King, the last Federalist ever to run for the presidency, 183 to 34. In fact, the Federalists carried only the states of Massachusetts, Connecticut, and Delaware. Daniel D. Tompkins of New York became Monroe's vice president.

Soon after the inauguration, Monroe and his wife traveled about the northern states on a goodwill tour. People responded nicely to the new President, waving from railroad stops and cheering along the riverbanks. This prompted the Boston *Columbian Centinel* to describe the trip as an "era of good feeling." The phrase, deserved or not, stuck to the Monroe administration for most of its eight years. It certainly helped the President. Although there were troubles aplenty, the young country was growing and feeling pretty good about itself. It may not have won the recent war, but it had stood toe to toe with mighty Britain. Expansion and good times were here. Friendly and presidential-looking, Monroe added to the country's sense of security and good feelings. Even John Quincy Adams, son of the second President and almost as cranky as his father, looked back on the Monroe years as the "golden age of this republic."

Indeed, the good feelings about Monroe even lasted through a depression. Secretary of the Treasury Alexander Hamilton, over Jefferson's objections, had established the first Bank of the United States in 1791. It lasted until 1811, when its charter ran out and was not renewed. The second Bank of the United States, founded in 1817, was badly managed, which helped to bring on the Panic of 1819 and its depression. But instead of getting mad at Monroe as a symbol of the government, those who lost money got mad at the bank. Monroe in the era of good feeling ran unopposed in 1820. Even so, his victory was not unanimous. One elector, William Plumer, voted against him because he said Monroe was a big spender. George Washington continues to be the only President elected unanimously.

James Monroe was not a President given to strong individual leadership. But merely competent or even mediocre Presidents, because of their personal charm, sometimes get undeserved credit. The reverse is also true. John Adams and his son, John

President Monroe, standing, discusses the Monroe Doctrine with his Cabinet. The Doctrine was announced at his annual message to Congress on December 2, 1823. John Quincy Adams is seated at the left; John C. Calhoun is the first man seated to the right of Monroe.

Quincy Adams, were both brilliant statesmen. However, they were ornery, not charming. They were also not popular and were not elected to second terms. They were the only two Presidents out of the first seven to serve just four years.

Monroe gets undeserved credit for the most important and famous event of his administration. Although it bears his name, the Monroe Doctrine was not written by Monroe nor was it his idea.

In his seventh annual message to Congress, December 2, 1823, the President forever changed the policy of the United States and gave himself added space in history books. He said, "The American continents, by the free and independent condition which they have assumed and maintain, are henceforth not to be considered as subjects for future colonization by any European powers."

Those words were taken from the papers of John Quincy Adams, Monroe's outstanding secretary of state. They stem from incidents concerning the U.S. boundaries. In 1821, the czar of Russia announced a new boundary for his Alaska territory. But the new boundary included land claimed by the United States in the Oregon Territory. When Monroe discussed this with his Cabinet, Adams said that America should contest any new "colonial establishments" from Europe. Monroe protested with Adams's words, and the czar backed down.

A year later, rumors said that Spain, with the help of France, was going to fight to regain its former colonies in Latin America. Most of them had been lost during the Napoleonic Wars. Great Britain, always anti-French, offered to sign a joint statement with the United States supporting the independent nations. When the President and U.S. government decided to consider the proposal, Adams objected. He said the United States should make its own policy, not follow someone else's. Hence the policy known as the Monroe Doctrine.

In effect, the Monroe Doctrine told all nations outside the Western Hemisphere to keep away—"America was for the Americans." It was a rather tough statement for a weak country with little means to back it up if challenged. But in fact, nobody paid much attention. Europe regarded the statement as "haughty." The Russian czar had already taken back his threat. Some countries in Latin America didn't even take it seriously, and some resented the United States setting itself up as the guardian of the New World.

Within a few decades, however, the United States would no longer be militarily weak. It would be ready to—and it did—back up the words of the Monroe Doctrine with action, not always to the delight of countries in South America.

The other big issue of the Monroe administration concerned the problem that nobody, including the President, wanted to deal with—slavery. Many in the North condemned the South for it, although sometimes in a whisper. After all, northerners were also guilty of shoddy treatment concerning black Americans. The South complained about shutting down the Atlantic slave trade in January 1808. However, slaveowners didn't complain too loudly since the law was often broken anyway, and trading slaves from state to state was still legal in most areas. Also, as the number of available imported slaves grew less, slave prices rose and many slaveowners profited.

A common scene in early nineteenth-century America was a group of slaves being brought to an auction for sale.

But now there was another serious problem. In 1819, Alabama had been admitted to the Union as the twenty-second state. This made a tidy arrangement of 11 slave states and 11 free states. Since both the House *and* the Senate had to pass a bill into law and since each state had only two senators each, everybody felt secure. Then along came Missouri. What was left of the Missouri Territory after Louisiana became a state in 1812 now applied to enter the Union as a slave state. The North began to grumble about slavery being extended west of the Mississippi River and about a new slave state in the Union. But by early 1820, the latter problem seemed solved because Maine, which had separated itself from Massachusetts, asked for statehood as a free state. And seemingly the whole business was solved when Henry Clay of Kentucky proposed the compromise that gave statehood to both Maine and Missouri. Maine would enter as a free state and Missouri as a slave state. However, slavery was to be banned in all territories west of Missouri's southern border, which meant the rest of the Louisiana Purchase. For that, Clay earned himself the title of "The Great Compromiser."

Just when it looked like everyone was pleased, there was another crisis. Before any new state could be admitted, Congress had to approve its constitution. But Missouri leaders slipped in a clause that said free blacks couldn't even enter the new state! In other words, a free black citizen living in New Jersey would not be allowed over the border into Missouri. That was contrary to the U.S. Constitution. Once more, Clay came to the rescue—or so it seemed. His second Missouri Compromise said that to be admitted, Missouri had to agree never to pass a law that violated the U.S. Constitution. But, of course, Missouri already *had* violated the Constitution. No one seemed to notice that, and Missouri became a state in 1821.

Actually, lots of people had noticed, including President Monroe, who, also like lots of people, did not have a better solution. A few leaders, including former President Jefferson, voiced their fear that this slavery issue was not solved. And in fact, it was not. The Missouri Compromise would be repealed in 1854 and declared unconstitutional in 1857. But the seeds of hatred it forced underground grew and festered and eventually helped to bring about the disaster that nearly did what powerful Great Britain could not do—destroy the young nation in the Civil War of 1861.

President James Monroe left office in 1826 after two full terms. Through his own efforts, some astute appointments, most notably the brilliant J.Q. Adams as secretary of state, and some good luck, he left the country stronger than before. It was also bigger. Expansion was probably the key achievement of the Monroe administration in spite of the strife it caused. At the end of his eight years, the number of states in the Union had jumped from 19 to 24, with the admission of Mississippi, Illinois, Alabama, Maine, and Missouri. The population had grown to about ten million. America's industrial revolution, sparked by the end of the War of 1812, was on the move. The Erie Canal, linking Buffalo, on Lake Erie, and Albany, on the Hudson River, was building. After it opened in 1825, produce and raw materials

The 363-mile Erie Canal, here shown being constructed at Lockport, New York, was funded completely by the state of New York at a cost of slightly more than $7 million.

from the west could sail down the Hudson to New York City, which would soon become one of the nation's, and the world's, great trade centers.

Besides proclaiming the Monroe Doctrine establishing America for Americans, Monroe sought to firm up fuzzy U.S. boundaries both north and south. With the Convention of 1818 in London, he settled the U.S.-Canadian border along the 49th parallel to the Rockies. Beyond that was the Oregon Territory, where both Americans and Canadians were to hold equal rights.

In the south, the Spanish were still holding eastern Florida. Monroe sent Secretary of State John Quincy Adams to talk to the Spanish minister about boundaries. In the meantime, the President nearly caused an international incident. Monroe gave permission to General Andrew Jackson to follow any Native American raiding parties over the border into Florida. Jackson was not above following orders according to his own rather liberal interpretation. He not only chased raiding parties, but he captured some Spanish forts and threw out the Spanish territorial governor.

The American public thought Jackson was a hero. Monroe was embarrassed by his flamboyant general, and Spain demanded an apology. Instead, Secretary Adams reasonably pointed out that Spain didn't have enough forces in the territory to hold it anyway. It took some persuasion, but the Spanish finally gave in and the United States got East and West Florida. Spain kept the territory of Texas but gave up rights to any claims in the Oregon Territory. Not a bad deal for $5 million! Now the United States controlled land from the Atlantic to the Rockies and had access to the Pacific through joint control of the Oregon Territory with Great Britain.

On the subject of money, the presidential salary in Monroe's time was $25,000 and would not be raised until 1873. To be sure, in those days that was a princely sum. However, except for repairs to the White House, Presidents had to pay for everything. That included servants and aides, all food and entertaining costs, as well as horses and carriages, even if used for official business! Until the administration of Warren G. Harding (1921–1923), if a President asked the queen of England to tea, for instance, it was his treat! Monroe, like Jefferson before him, was in debt when he left the White House in 1825. Obviously, leaders in the those early years did not serve for financial gain.

Monroe and his wife retired to their Oak Hill, Virginia, home, which was designed by Thomas Jefferson. In 1829, Monroe served as the presiding officer of the Virginia Constitutional Convention, but otherwise lived quietly until Elizabeth died in 1830. By then Monroe was in poor health and still without much money. He sold his home and moved to New York City to live with his daughter. There he died in 1831, the third—and so far the last—United States President to die on the Fourth of July. Not yet 60 when he took office in 1817, James Monroe was the last Revolutionary War patriot and the last eighteenth-century figure to lead the nation.

Names in the News in Monroe's Time

John C. Calhoun (1782–1850):

Yale graduate, brilliant congressman from South Carolina, Monroe's secretary of war (1817–1825), vice president under John Quincy Adams. Favored a strong military and a strong national bank. After Panic of 1819, when cotton prices fell, Calhoun became a fervent defender of states' rights for the South.

Henry Clay (1777–1852):

Born in Virginia, moved to Lexington, Kentucky, where he became a lawyer. A perennial candidate for the presidency, his efforts to bring about the Missouri Compromise of 1820 earned him the title "The Great Compromiser."

Rufus King (1755–1827):

Harvard graduate and brilliant orator. Elected as senator from New York, he lost the 1816 presidential election to Monroe as the last of the Federalist candidates. U.S. minister to Great Britain; called one of the most effective ambassadors the nation ever had.

Maria Hester Monroe and Samuel Gouverneur:

In 1820, Monroe's 16-year-old daughter Maria and his White House secretary, Samuel Gouverneur, became husband and wife in the first marriage performed in the White House.

Chapter Six

J.Q. "Old Man Eloquent" Adams

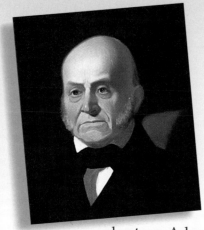

John Quincy Adams (1825-1829)

*H*e was not known as "Old Man Eloquent" until he was out of the White House, but John Quincy Adams earned the title long before that. A most articulate speaker, he was brilliant and absolutely tireless when duty called. He was, in short, an Adams, part of the only U.S. father-son combination, at least so far, to become President. Adams the son was remarkably like Adams the father: austere, tight-lipped, sensitive, irritable, abrupt, stubborn, and vain. He was, alas, not a popular figure. He was, however, a great statesman and steadfast in his devotion to his country. He was also convinced that he knew what was best for the United States.

John Quincy Adams may well have known himself better than anyone else. He once said, "I am a man of reserved, cold, austere, and forbidding manners." He added that even though he knew of this defect of character, "I have not the pliability to reform it."

The second of four children, he was born to John and Abigail on July 11, 1767, in Braintree (now Quincy), Massachusetts. Growing up in a time of increasing trouble with Great Britain, such as the Battle of Bunker Hill in 1775, Adams would be forever suspicious of the British. By the time he was a teenager, he had traveled about Europe with his father, spoke several languages, and had studied in Paris and Amsterdam. In 1785, he returned to the United States and enrolled at Harvard College, which he found exceedingly dull. That may have prompted him to study extra hard, for he graduated in two years, passed the bar in 1790, and began practicing law in Boston.

By the time John Quincy was 27 years old, he had impressed President George Washington with his many political articles. Against the wishes of Adams Senior, who was worried about charges of favoritism, Washington appointed the younger Adams minister to the Netherlands. On one of his official trips to London, Adams met Louisa Catherine Johnson, the daughter of the American consul general. They were married in July 1797, after John Quincy's father had become the second U.S. President. They had four children: George Washington, John, Charles Francis, and Louisa Catherine.

Louisa Catherine Adams

Left to his father, John Quincy's political career might well have died after service in the Netherlands. President Adams was overly sensitive to charges of favoring his son. It took a retired George Washington to tell Adams that the very capable John Quincy would be an asset to the government. Actually, his father already knew that and appointed his son minister to Prussia in 1797. He served admirably if uneventfully and came home in 1801.

Adams was elected to the Massachusetts State Senate in 1802 and a year later was sent to the U.S. Senate, where his independent voting record annoyed many at home who had voted for him. He stayed in the Senate until 1808, although he spent some time teaching at Harvard in 1805. In 1809, President Madison appointed him minister to Russia (1809–1811) and, in 1814, a commissioner in Ghent, Belgium, to help work out the peace treaty that ended the War of 1812. Strangely enough, the anti-British Adams was then asked to become minister to Great

John Quincy Adams, U.S. commissioner in Ghent, Belgium, shakes hands with the British representative, in uniform, Sir James Gambier, at the signing of the Treaty of Ghent, on Christmas Eve, 1814.

Britain. Stranger still, he agreed and stayed in London until he was called home in 1817 to become Monroe's secretary of state.

John Quincy Adams was a superb secretary of state, possibly the best ever. He was a master administrator and a tireless worker. He was largely responsible for the successes of the Monroe administration: settlement of the Canada-U.S. border dispute, the treaty that gave Spanish Florida to the United States, the stand against Russian claims to the Oregon Territory, and, of course, the Monroe Doctrine. Even his dislike of the British did not prevent him from forging alliances that forever bound Great Britain and the United States in friendship.

The State Department under Adams ran like a well-oiled machine. President Monroe deserves at least a little credit for the department's success just because he appointed Adams and thoroughly supported him.

After Monroe, it might have seemed natural for John Quincy Adams to get the presidential nomination. But distinguished service was no match for a cranky personality. Adams had made few friends in Washington. So in 1824, the Democratic-Republicans gave the nod to William H. Crawford of Georgia. The party, however, was badly split and different sections of the country wanted their own candidates. By election day, three other candidates were also on the ballot: Henry Clay of

Kentucky, Andrew Jackson of Tennessee, and John Quincy Adams of Massachusetts. John C. Calhoun represented the South. He knew he could not win the election so he chose to run, instead, for vice president. None of the other candidates wanted to antagonize the South, so Calhoun ran unopposed for the second slot.

In the election of 1824, not one of the four candidates received a majority of the electoral votes. Jackson had 99; Adams, 84; Crawford, who suffered a paralyzing stroke during the campaign, 41; and Clay, 37. That threw the election into the House of Representatives. Since only the three highest names could be considered, Clay was out. Crawford was too ill. That left Jackson and Adams.

Clay didn't think highly of Adams, but he thought even less of Jackson. Referring to Jackson's victory in the War of 1812, Clay said, "I cannot believe that killing 2,500 Englishmen at New Orleans qualifies him for the duties of the presidency." So, Clay pledged his support to Adams and then persuaded several states to do likewise. The final count of states was Adams, 13 votes, Jackson, 7, and Crawford, 4. In this manner, John Quincy Adams, at age 57, became the sixth President of the United States, with John C. Calhoun of South Carolina as vice president.

When President Adams announced his Cabinet choices, Henry Clay was named secretary of state. Andrew Jackson and all his supporters were furious! Foul, they cried, a corrupt bargain has been struck! Was there a secret bargain between the two? The presidency in exchange for secretary of state? No one knows for sure. Even so, according to Adams's diary, he thought Clay was the best man for the job. Whatever the truth, it was a bad political move. Jackson's growing supporters gained control of both houses of Congress in 1826. They yelled "corruption" at every opportunity and tried to block the President's every move during his four years in office. During the four years of the Adams administration, however, the Jacksonians in Congress began to disagree among themselves. The Jacksonians called themselves the party of the common people and were against too much federal power. The anti-Jacksonians called for justice for Native Americans, among other things, as did Adams. This did not mean, however, that the anti-Jacksonians were any more friends of the Native American than were Jackson's followers. Neither side wanted Native Americans on the political scene. Anti-Jacksonians believed that the right to vote should depend on adequate wealth and education, which they felt all Americans should have. This group began to call themselves National Republicans. Soon, the country once again had two distinct political parties.

After a brilliant career in Congress, Adams really didn't do much as President. Some failures can be chalked up to his enemies, some to his own uncompromising personality. He did show true vision for the country with his proposals for farsighted improvements: government aid to education; a national network of roads and canals; a naval academy; a plan to map the country; a new department, to be called Interior, to protect

natural resources. Eventually, all these things were done. Not one of them during the Adams administration. The anti-Adams Congress defeated every one.

The President didn't even do well in foreign affairs, where he'd been so brilliant during the Monroe administration. Soon after Adams took office, Simon Bolívar called for a conference of American nations to be held in Panama. Bolívar had liberated many Latin American regions

Simon Bolívar, who fought for the independence of Colombia, Venezuela, Ecuador, Peru, and Bolivia from Spain, wanted to establish a union of newly freed Latin American nations with the aid of the United States.

from colonial control, and he was a great hero. Adams was asked to send two delegates to the conference.

Instead of just doing it, the President first asked the approval of Congress. But Congress's approval wasn't necessary. He could have done it on his own. What he got was a hornet's nest. The South didn't want the United States at the conference for fear the issue of slavery would come up. Northern leaders wanted to go because it might be good for export trade. Some congressmen were against the United States at *any* international conference— period. All this wrangling took about four months while Adams waited for the approval he didn't need. Finally, Congress said yes and the President named two representatives. One of them died on the way to Panama, and the other hadn't even left home when the conference ended.

Adams also got into an international ruckus, perhaps not surprisingly, with Great Britain. Americans had long wanted the British to open up trade with their West Indian possessions. At last, in 1825, the British relented enough to open the trade doors at least a crack. That wasn't enough for the American President. After ignoring the offer for about a year, Adams told his minister in London to ask for better terms. Naturally, the British were miffed and withdrew. Once again, they closed the door to U.S. trade with the West Indies. Not surprisingly, the American business community was also miffed and blamed Adams.

Even when Adams supported the highest ideals, he seemed to be on the opposite side of the voting public. Always antislavery, he also deplored U.S. treatment of Native Americans. As some sort of compensation, he asked Congress to set aside western lands for the tribes and to guarantee them certain rights. Congress said no. Adams may have wanted the Native Americans to be "out of sight," but the popular attitude of the day was more on the order of Andrew Jackson's handling of the "Indian problem" in Florida—out of the country is even better than out of sight.

As if to prove he could antagonize even more U.S. voting citizens, Adams mishandled the so-called Tariff of Abominations of 1828. He wanted the Congress to pass a reasonable tariff, or tax, on certain goods coming into the country. Instead, every region began yelling for its own cause. The manufacturing Northeast wanted a high tax on foreign-made manufactured goods. Kentucky raised hemp, so naturally it wanted a high tax on hemp raised elsewhere. The silk mills of New Hampshire had the same idea about silk. Adams simply refused to wade into the mess. He said he'd go along with whatever Congress passed. This was not a good move. Congress passed an absurdly high tariff. What could Adams do? He had to sign it. In doing so, he assured himself that the South, furiously against the bill, would never vote for him again. It didn't.

In the next presidential election, lots of electors didn't vote for him either. The highly popular General Andrew Jackson of Tennessee easily won the election of 1828, 178 electoral votes to 83. Of course, Adams didn't help his cause by refusing to campaign. He felt it was beneath his dignity. So, just like his father, he behaved with well-mannered restraint and kept his mouth shut. Also just like his father, he wanted but failed to get a second term.

It was apparently not in the Adamses' nature to accept defeat gracefully. John Adams had left town before Jefferson's inauguration. John Quincy did likewise before Jackson was sworn in.

Aloof and stubborn, John Quincy's personality helped to shorten his time in the White House. But he had some successes, too, such as favorable commercial agreements with European countries and the building of the Chesapeake and Ohio Canal, one of the few projects he got through Congress. Despite charges of a corrupt bargain with Clay, his character was generally accepted as incorruptible. He and his charming wife presided over stately and gracious social functions at the White House. Yet, the Adamses were both so reserved and kept so out of the limelight that not many people outside of Washington knew anything about them. Back home in Massachusetts, Adams was elected to the House of Representatives in 1830. He was overjoyed to be back in office once again. His mind and his spirit were reborn. He was a leader in establishing the Smithsonian Institution in Washington, D.C. He fought to make education available to all Americans. He is responsible for ending the so-called Gag Rules in Congress. In 1836, the House passed the first

The only U.S. President to run for public office after his defeat for reelection, Adams suffered a stroke in the U.S. Senate on February 21, 1848.

of several resolutions that would not allow the discussion of antislavery petitions. Adams said that was against the Constitution. Although ignored for years, he persisted, badgering his fellow congressmen until the Gag Rules where abolished in 1844.

Sometimes Adams even agreed with President Jackson's side. He still carried a grudge, though. When Jackson received an honorary degree at Harvard, Adams refused to attend the ceremony.

In 1846, the grand old patriot suffered a stroke. He was back at work within four months. When he walked feebly into the House, the whole chamber stood as one. They may have rarely agreed with him, but they knew a statesman when they saw one. Two years later, on February 21, 1848, Adams suffered a second stroke, this time at his desk. He died two days later.

In truth, considering the brilliance and devotion to duty of John Quincy Adams, he could have been, and should have been, a great President. He wasn't. His own personality and changing times just got in the way. A statesman he surely was, but his greatest contributions to his country took place across the city from the White House, especially during the last 17 years of his life spent in the Congress of the United States.

Names in the News in J.Q. Adams's Time

Thomas Hart Benton (1782–1858):

Congressional leader from North Carolina, spokesman for the west, and a staunch Adams political foe. However, when the ex-President died while in Congress, Benton admiringly said, "Where could death have found him but at the post of duty?"

William H. Crawford (1772–1834):

Senator from Georgia, secretary of the treasury (1816–1825) under Monroe. He became the most prominent southern politician of his time, supported by both Jefferson and Madison. Had he not become paralyzed in 1823, he might well have become the nation's sixth President instead of John Quincy Adams.

John Randolph (1773–1833):

Congressman from Virginia, brilliant, flamboyant, often obscene. His disturbed temperament gave way to insanity late in life. With slashing wit, he said of the sixth President, "I bore some humble part in putting down the dynasty of John the First. I hope to aid in putting down the dynasty of John the Second." And so he did.

A brilliant orator, John Randolph is shown here with his hunting dogs and his congressman's desk.

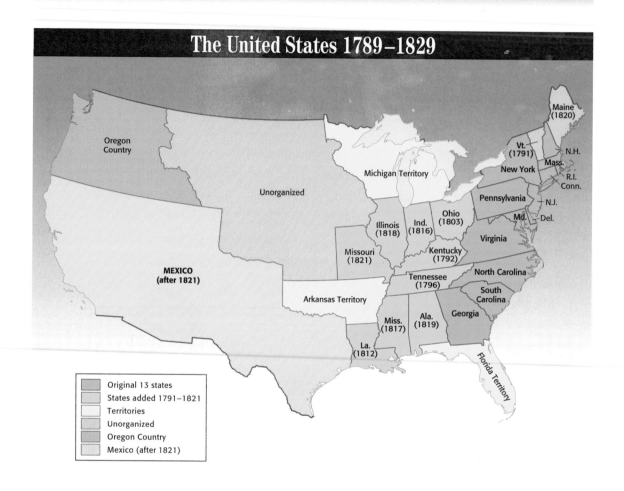

By 1829 most of the states east of the Mississippi River
had the boundaries they still have today.

Important Facts and Events in the Terms

of Presidents One Through Six

1. George Washington (1789–1797)

Federalist; age at inauguration, 57

Born: Pope's Creek (Wakefield), Virginia, February 22, 1732

Died: Mount Vernon, Virginia, December 14, 1799

Education; occupation: Private tutors; planter, soldier

Military service: Virginia militia, 1752–1758; commander, Continental
Army, 1775–1783

Family: Martha Dandridge Custis (married 1759)

Important events during Washington's terms:

1789: State, War, and Treasury Departments created;
Bill of Rights (first ten Amendments) passed.

1790: U.S. Supreme Court holds first session.

1791: Vermont becomes 14th state.

1792: Kentucky becomes 15th state.

1793: Citizen Genét affair

1794: Whiskey Rebellion

1795: Jay Treaty with Great Britain ratified.

1796: Tennessee becomes 16th state;
Washington's Farewell Address

2. John Adams (1797–1801)

Federalist party; age at inauguration, 61

Born: Braintree (Quincy), Massachusetts, October 19, 1735

Died: Quincy, Massachusetts, July 4, 1826

Education; occupation: Harvard (M.A., 1758); lawyer

Family: Abigail Smith (married 1758); children: John Quincy,
Susanna, Charles, Thomas Boylston

Important events during Adams's term:

1797: X,Y,Z Affair

1798: 11th Amendment (on judicial power) ratified;
Department of the Navy and Marine Corps created;
Alien and Sedition Acts signed.

1800: Seat of government moves from Philadelphia to
Washington, D.C.;
Adams becomes first President to occupy White House.

3. Thomas Jefferson (1801–1809)

Democratic-Republican party; age at inauguration, 57
Born: Shadwell, Virginia, April 13, 1743
Died: Monticello, Virginia, July 4, 1826
Education; occupation: College of William and Mary (1762); lawyer
Family: Martha Wayles Skelton (married 1772); children: Martha,
Maria, Lucy Elizabeth
Important events during Jefferson's terms:

1801: Tripoli declares war on U.S.

1802: Ohio becomes 17th state.

1803: Louisiana purchased from France for $15 million;
Supreme Court decides *Marbury v. Madison*

1804: Lewis and Clark expedition leaves St. Louis for the west;
12th Amendment (on presidential electors) ratified.

1805: U.S. signs peace treaty with Tripoli.

1807: Embargo Act passes.

1808: Importing African slaves is prohibited.

4. James Madison (1809–1817)

Democratic-Republican party; age at inauguration, 57
Born: Port Conway, Virginia, March 16, 1751
Died: Montpelier, Virginia, June 28, 1836

Education; occupation: Princeton (1771); lawyer

Family: Dorothea (Dolley) Payne Todd (married 1794)

Important events during Madison's terms:

    1809: Embargo Act replaced by Non-Intercourse Act.

    1811: Battle of Tippecanoe

    1812: Louisiana becomes 18th state;
          war begins with Great Britain.

    1813: Commodore Perry victorious on Lake Erie.

    1814: White House burned by British; "The Star Spangled
          Banner" composed by Francis Scott Key;
          war with Great Britain ends.

    1815: Battle of New Orleans

    1816: Indiana becomes 19th state.

5. James Monroe (1817–1825)

Democratic-Republican party; age at inauguration, 58

Born: Westmoreland County, Virginia, April 18, 1758

Died: New York City, July 4, 1831

Education; occupation: College of William and Mary (1776); lawyer

Military service: Third Virginia Regiment, Continental Army
   (1776–1779)

Family: Elizabeth Kortright (married 1786); children: Eliza, Maria Hester

Important events during Monroe's terms:

    1817: Mississippi becomes 20th state.

    1818: Illinois becomes 21st state.

    1819: Alabama becomes 22nd state;
          Panic of 1819

    1820: Missouri Compromise;
          Maine becomes 23rd state;
          U.S. acquires Florida from Spain.

    1821: Missouri becomes 24th state.

    1823: Monroe Doctrine proclaimed.

6. John Quincy Adams (1825–1829)

Democratic-Republican party, age at inauguration, 57

Born: Braintree (Quincy), Massachusetts, July 11, 1767

Died: Washington, D.C., February 23, 1848

Education; occupation: Harvard (1787); lawyer

Family: Louisa Catherine Johnson (married 1797); children: George Washington, John, Charles Francis, Louisa Catherine

Important events during Adams's term:

1825: Erie Canal opens.

1826: John Adams and Thomas Jefferson die on July 4; 50th anniversary of signing of Declaration of Independence.

1828: Work begins on Baltimore and Ohio Railroad; "Tariff of Abominations" passes.

Glossary

abolition In the early years of U.S. government, used mainly to refer to putting an end to slavery.

administration A term of office, usually of the executive branch of government. Washington's administration lasted two terms, or eight years. Except for F. D. Roosevelt, no President has served more than two terms.

alien A foreign-born person who has not been naturalized.

aristocrat One with the bearing and viewpoint of the privileged or noble classes.

Cabinet A group of people selected by the President who serve as advisers and head up departments of the government.

Commander in Chief The supreme head of an armed force.

doctrine A statement of government policy, as the Monroe Doctrine.

dumbwaiter A small platform raised or lowered on a continuous belt; used to bring food from one floor of a building to another.

elector One qualified to vote in an election; particularly a member of the Electoral College.

Electoral College The body of electors that votes for President and vice president of the United States. Electors were originally intended to be chosen by state legislatures. Today, voters indicate choice for President and vice president; then, winning party's electors cast each state's votes for candidates chosen.

eloquent When referring to a speaker, marks one as forceful, vivid, and moving.

embargo Government order that prohibits commercial ships from leaving port; a legal stop on commerce.

inauguration Ceremony in which the President takes the oath of office.

legacy Something of value left behind or bequeathed from an ancestor or predecessor.

militia In early years, referred to a group of male citizens subject to call to military service.

minister A diplomatic representative of one nation to another; usually has the rank below an ambassador but can also be equal to an ambassador.

naturalization The act of becoming a citizen of a country in which one was not born.

obelisk Upright, four-sided pillar that usually ends in a pyramid at the top, as the Washington Monument.

pantaloons Wide trousers that generally went out of style early in the nineteenth century.

patriot One who loves his or her country and supports its interests. In the struggle against the British, one who fought for independence.

radical In government, used to describe someone who calls for extreme changes to existing practices.

ratification Approval of a legislative body especially of an act or treaty.

sedition Resistance to lawful authority; incitement to insurrection.

tariff In U.S., charges imposed by a government on imported or exported goods.

treason Overt attempt to overthrow the government; in the U.S., punishable by death in wartime.

treaty A contract between the governing bodies of two or more nations, usually ratified by a legislative body.

tribute Payment from one nation to another often for protection; a gift showing respect for service.

Further Reading

Barton, David. *The Bulletproof George Washington*. Wallbuilders, Inc., 1990

Bober, Natalie S. *Abigail Adams: Witness to a Revolution*. Simon & Schuster Childrens, 1995

Bosco, Peter I. *War of 1812*. Millbrook Press, 1991

Faber, Harold and Faber, Doris. *We the People: The Story of the United States Constitution since 1787*. Simon & Schuster Childrens, 1987

Favors, John and Favors, Kathryne. *John Quincy Adams and the Armistad: A President Who Fought for the Rights of Africans*. Jonka Enterprises, no date

Fritz, Jean. *The Great Little Madison*. Putnam, 1989

Green, Carl and Sanford, William. *Presidency*. Rourke Corp., 1990

Harness, Cheryl. *The Amazing Impossible Erie Canal*. Simon & Schuster Childrens, 1995

Kronenwetter, Michael. *The Supreme Court of the United States*. Enslow, 1995

Leas, Allan. *Abolition of the Slave Trade*. Trafalgar Square, 1989

Lindop, Edmund. *Birth of the Constitution*. Enslow, 1987

Lossing, B.J. *Lives of the Signers of the Declaration of Independence*. Wallbuilders, 1995

Marsh, Joan. *Martha Washington*. Franklin Watts, 1993

Meltzer, Milton. *Bill of Rights: How We Got It and What It Means*. Harper Collins, 1990

———. *The Revolutionary Aristocrat*. Franklin Watts, 1991

Shorto, Russell. *Tecumseh*. Silver Burdett Press, 1989

Stallones, Jared. *Zebulon Pike and the Explorers of the American West*. Chelsea House, 1992

Twist, Clint. *Lewis and Clark: Exploring North America*. Raintree Steck-Vaughn, 1994

Waters, Kate. *The Story of the White House*. Scholastic, 1991

Weiss, Ann E. *Supreme Court*. Enslow, 1987

Wetzel, Charles. *James Monroe*. Chelsea House, 1989

Index

Numbers in **bold** indicate pictures.